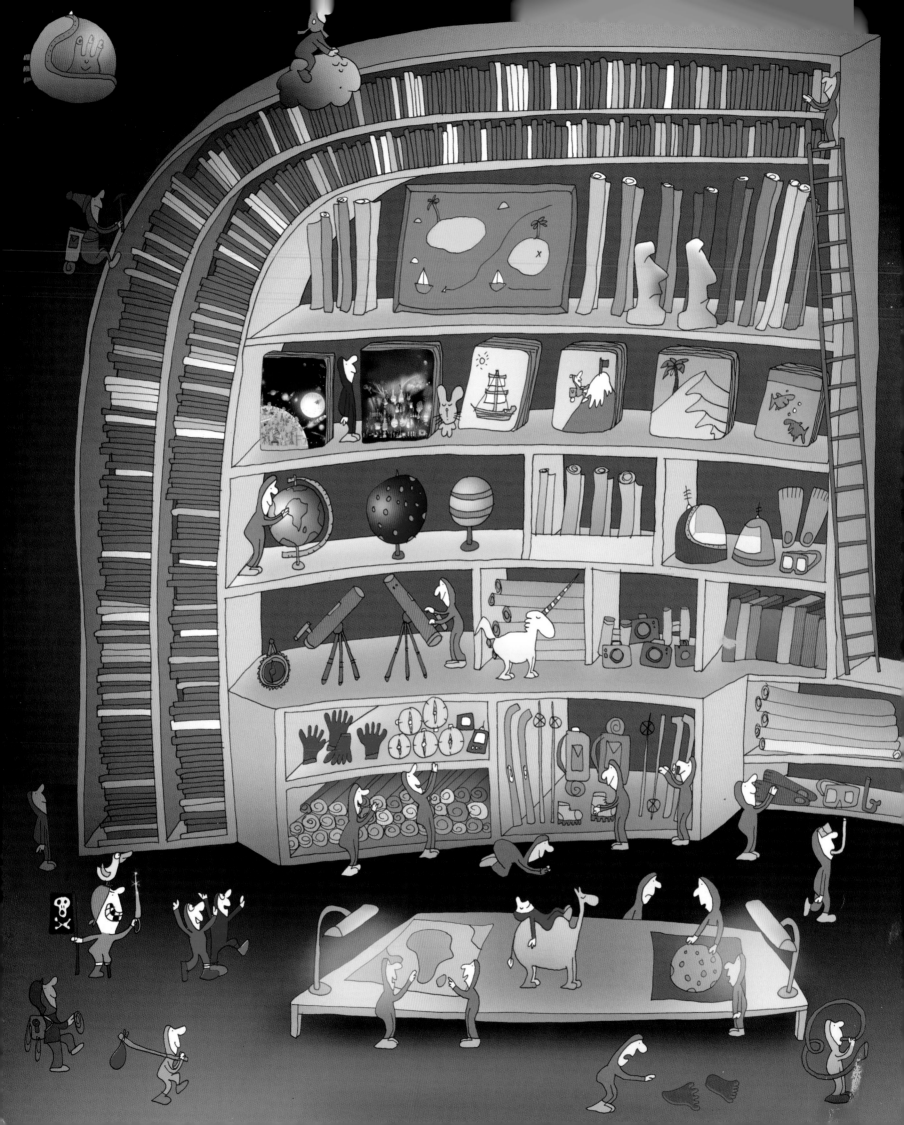

THE MOST BRILLIANT
BOLDLY GOING BOOK OF
EXPLORATION EVER
by the Brainwaves

Illustrated by Lisa Swerling and Ralph Lazar
Written by Peter Chrisp

DK

London, New York, Melbourne,
Munich, and Delhi

Senior Editor Andrea Mills
Senior Art Editor Jim Green
Editor Steven Carton
Designer Katie Knutton

Managing Editor Linda Esposito
Managing Art Editor Diane Thistlethwaite

Consultant Philip Parker

Cartographic assistance Ed Merritt,
Simon Mumford

Publishing Manager Andrew Macintyre
Category Publisher Laura Buller

Production Editor Andy Hilliard
Senior Production Controller Angela Graef

Jacket Editor Joanna Pocock

First published in the United States in 2010
by DK Publishing
375 Hudson Street, New York, New York 10014

Copyright © 2010 Dorling Kindersley Limited
A Penguin Company

10 11 12 13 14 10 9 8 7 6 5 4 3 2 1
177819—02/10

A catalog record for this book is available
from the Library of Congress.

ISBN: 978-0-75666-290-5

Color reproduction by
Media Development Printing Ltd.

Printed and bound by LEO, China

Discover more at
www.dk.com
www.thebrainwaves.com

NOV 2 7 2010

CONTENTS

Exploring the world

As long as there have been people, there have been explorers. In prehistoric times, people managed to settle almost every inhabitable part of the planet. Yet for most of our history, the human race was divided into many regions, with people in one part of the world completely unaware of distant lands. It has only been in the last few thousands years that explorers have recorded their discoveries. Thanks to their writings and maps, an accurate picture of the world was created.

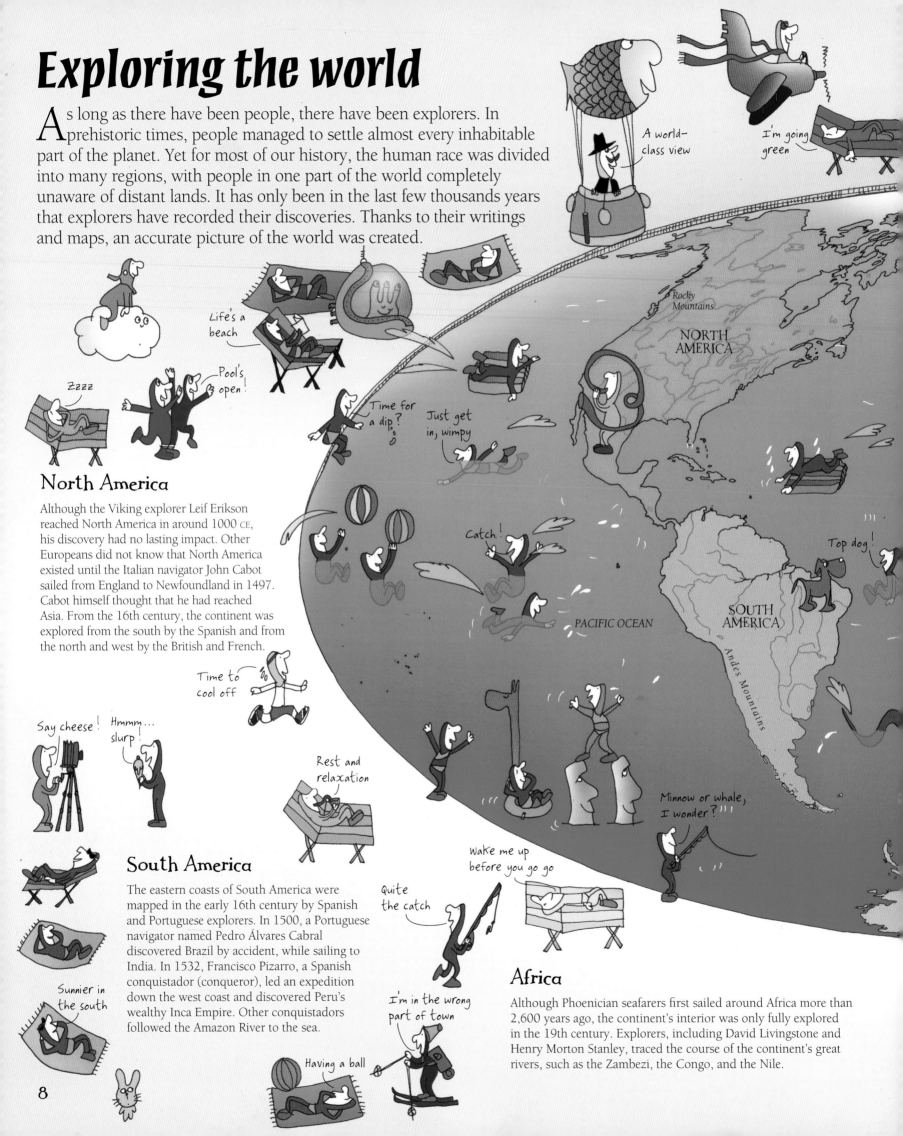

A world-class view

I'm going green

Life's a beach

Pool's open!

Zzzz

Time for a dip?

Just get in, wimpy

Catch!

Top dog!

Rocky Mountains

NORTH AMERICA

PACIFIC OCEAN

SOUTH AMERICA

Andes Mountains

North America

Although the Viking explorer Leif Erikson reached North America in around 1000 CE, his discovery had no lasting impact. Other Europeans did not know that North America existed until the Italian navigator John Cabot sailed from England to Newfoundland in 1497. Cabot himself thought that he had reached Asia. From the 16th century, the continent was explored from the south by the Spanish and from the north and west by the British and French.

Time to cool off

Say cheese!

Hmmm... slurp!

Rest and relaxation

Wake me up before you go go

Quite the catch

Minnow or whale, I wonder?

South America

The eastern coasts of South America were mapped in the early 16th century by Spanish and Portuguese explorers. In 1500, a Portuguese navigator named Pedro Álvares Cabral discovered Brazil by accident, while sailing to India. In 1532, Francisco Pizarro, a Spanish conquistador (conqueror), led an expedition down the west coast and discovered Peru's wealthy Inca Empire. Other conquistadors followed the Amazon River to the sea.

Sunnier in the south

I'm in the wrong part of town

Having a ball

Africa

Although Phoenician seafarers first sailed around Africa more than 2,600 years ago, the continent's interior was only fully explored in the 19th century. Explorers, including David Livingstone and Henry Morton Stanley, traced the course of the continent's great rivers, such as the Zambezi, the Congo, and the Nile.

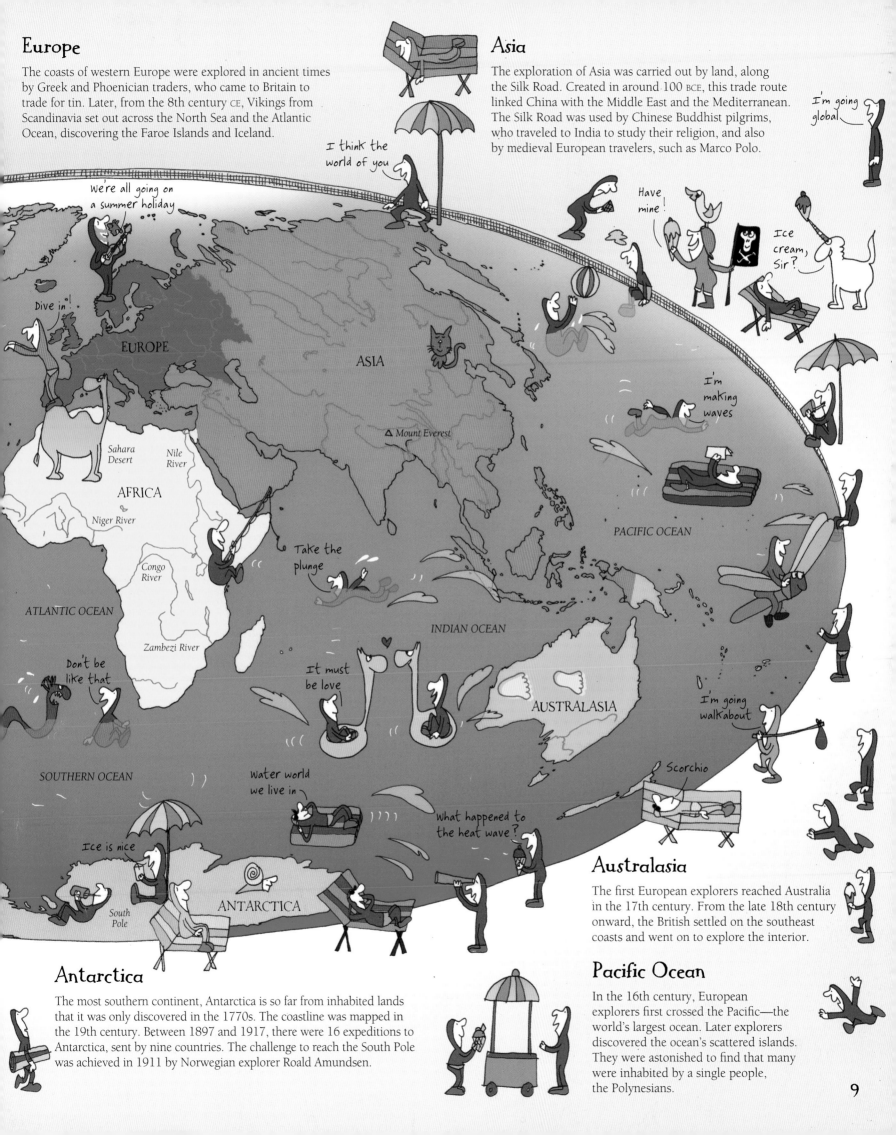

Europe

The coasts of western Europe were explored in ancient times by Greek and Phoenician traders, who came to Britain to trade for tin. Later, from the 8th century CE, Vikings from Scandinavia set out across the North Sea and the Atlantic Ocean, discovering the Faroe Islands and Iceland.

Asia

The exploration of Asia was carried out by land, along the Silk Road. Created in around 100 BCE, this trade route linked China with the Middle East and the Mediterranean. The Silk Road was used by Chinese Buddhist pilgrims, who traveled to India to study their religion, and also by medieval European travelers, such as Marco Polo.

Australasia

The first European explorers reached Australia in the 17th century. From the late 18th century onward, the British settled on the southeast coasts and went on to explore the interior.

Antarctica

The most southern continent, Antarctica is so far from inhabited lands that it was only discovered in the 1770s. The coastline was mapped in the 19th century. Between 1897 and 1917, there were 16 expeditions to Antarctica, sent by nine countries. The challenge to reach the South Pole was achieved in 1911 by Norwegian explorer Roald Amundsen.

Pacific Ocean

In the 16th century, European explorers first crossed the Pacific—the world's largest ocean. Later explorers discovered the ocean's scattered islands. They were astonished to find that many were inhabited by a single people, the Polynesians.

9

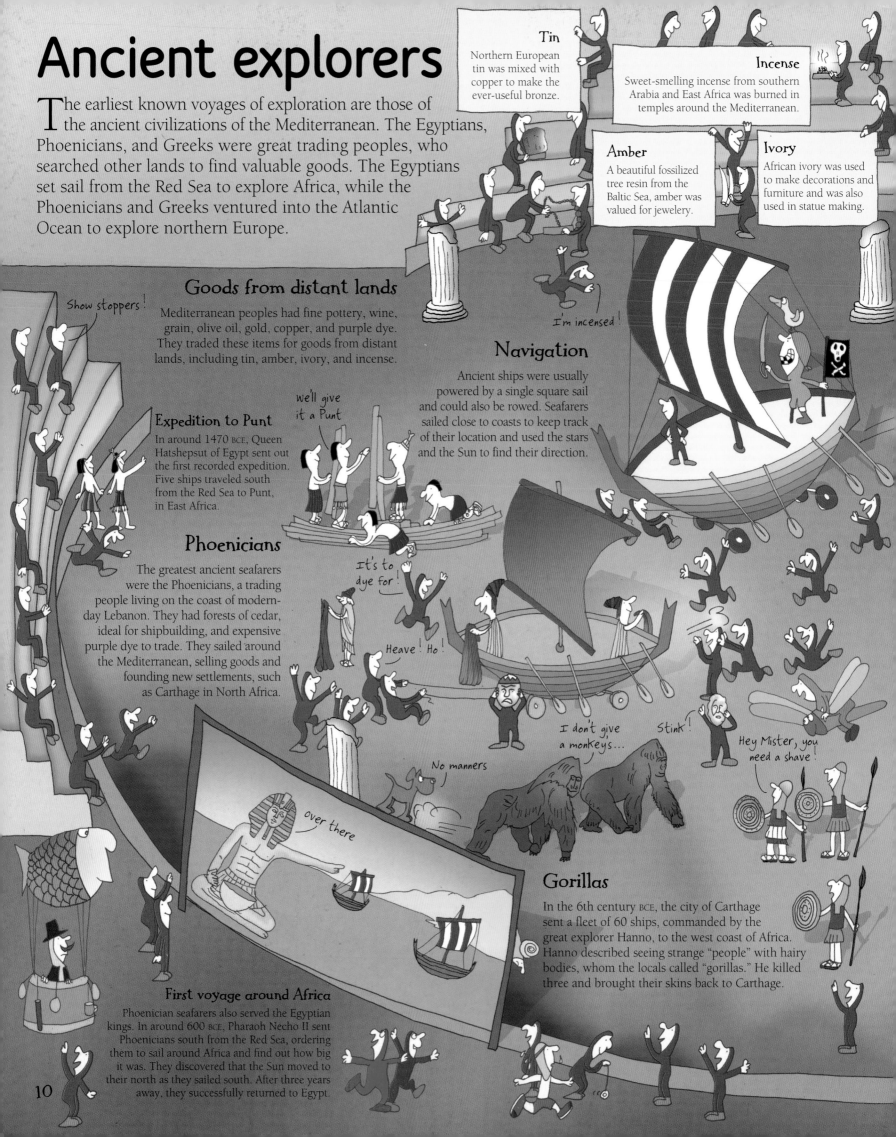

Ancient explorers

The earliest known voyages of exploration are those of the ancient civilizations of the Mediterranean. The Egyptians, Phoenicians, and Greeks were great trading peoples, who searched other lands to find valuable goods. The Egyptians set sail from the Red Sea to explore Africa, while the Phoenicians and Greeks ventured into the Atlantic Ocean to explore northern Europe.

Tin
Northern European tin was mixed with copper to make the ever-useful bronze.

Incense
Sweet-smelling incense from southern Arabia and East Africa was burned in temples around the Mediterranean.

Amber
A beautiful fossilized tree resin from the Baltic Sea, amber was valued for jewelery.

Ivory
African ivory was used to make decorations and furniture and was also used in statue making.

Goods from distant lands

Mediterranean peoples had fine pottery, wine, grain, olive oil, gold, copper, and purple dye. They traded these items for goods from distant lands, including tin, amber, ivory, and incense.

Expedition to Punt

In around 1470 BCE, Queen Hatshepsut of Egypt sent out the first recorded expedition. Five ships traveled south from the Red Sea to Punt, in East Africa.

Phoenicians

The greatest ancient seafarers were the Phoenicians, a trading people living on the coast of modern-day Lebanon. They had forests of cedar, ideal for shipbuilding, and expensive purple dye to trade. They sailed around the Mediterranean, selling goods and founding new settlements, such as Carthage in North Africa.

Navigation

Ancient ships were usually powered by a single square sail and could also be rowed. Seafarers sailed close to coasts to keep track of their location and used the stars and the Sun to find their direction.

Gorillas

In the 6th century BCE, the city of Carthage sent a fleet of 60 ships, commanded by the great explorer Hanno, to the west coast of Africa. Hanno described seeing strange "people" with hairy bodies, whom the locals called "gorillas." He killed three and brought their skins back to Carthage.

First voyage around Africa

Phoenician seafarers also served the Egyptian kings. In around 600 BCE, Pharaoh Necho II sent Phoenicians south from the Red Sea, ordering them to sail around Africa and find out how big it was. They discovered that the Sun moved to their north as they sailed south. After three years away, they successfully returned to Egypt.

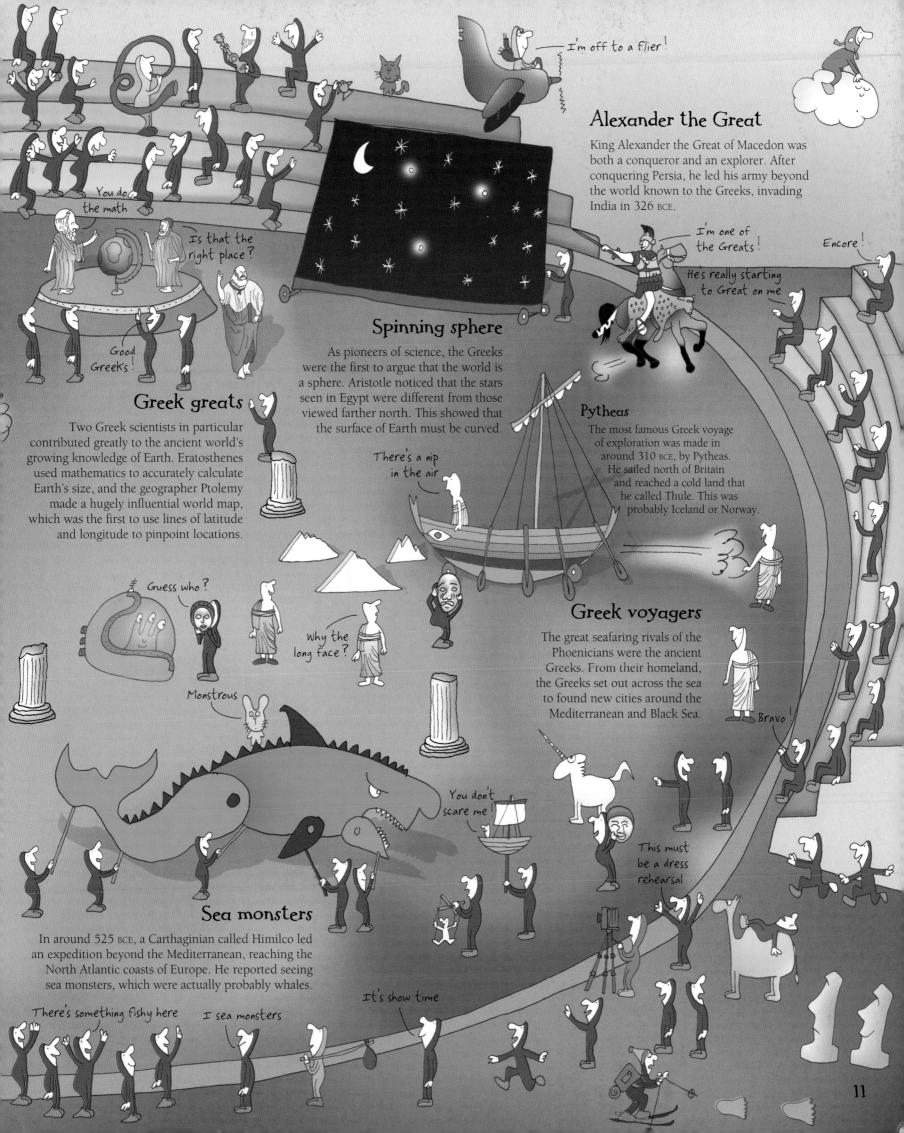

Alexander the Great

King Alexander the Great of Macedon was both a conqueror and an explorer. After conquering Persia, he led his army beyond the world known to the Greeks, invading India in 326 BCE.

Spinning sphere

As pioneers of science, the Greeks were the first to argue that the world is a sphere. Aristotle noticed that the stars seen in Egypt were different from those viewed farther north. This showed that the surface of Earth must be curved.

Greek greats

Two Greek scientists in particular contributed greatly to the ancient world's growing knowledge of Earth. Eratosthenes used mathematics to accurately calculate Earth's size, and the geographer Ptolemy made a hugely influential world map, which was the first to use lines of latitude and longitude to pinpoint locations.

Pytheas

The most famous Greek voyage of exploration was made in around 310 BCE, by Pytheas. He sailed north of Britain and reached a cold land that he called Thule. This was probably Iceland or Norway.

Greek voyagers

The great seafaring rivals of the Phoenicians were the ancient Greeks. From their homeland, the Greeks set out across the sea to found new cities around the Mediterranean and Black Sea.

Sea monsters

In around 525 BCE, a Carthaginian called Himilco led an expedition beyond the Mediterranean, reaching the North Atlantic coasts of Europe. He reported seeing sea monsters, which were actually probably whales.

11

VIKING VOYAGES

The greatest seafarers of the early Middle Ages were the Vikings, the people of Scandinavia. From the late 8th century CE, they set off in all directions, to raid, trade, and settle new lands. They traveled east and south along the rivers of Russia to the Black Sea, as well as heading west into the North Sea and Atlantic Ocean. There they found Iceland and Greenland and became the first Europeans to reach North America.

Routes taken by the Vikings
_c. 790–1100 CE_

Icelandic sagas

The stories of the Viking voyages of exploration were written down in Iceland, in books called sagas. These were composed for entertainment. On long, dark evenings, Icelanders loved to hear the stories of the voyages of their brave ancestors.

YOUR JOURNEY BEGINS THIS WAY

Viking ships

Voyages were made in double-ended oak ships, with a single square sail. There were several types of these ships, but the best known was the longship, with a dragon figurehead. This slim, fast vessel was used in sea battles. For trading and exploring, people used a bigger bellied ship called a "knarr."

Where was Vinland?

Although Vinland must have been in North America, we do not know exactly where it was. The only Norse settlement that was discovered was in Newfoundland, but grapes do not grow there. Vinland may have been farther south, where grapes could grow, or perhaps the Vikings mistook berries for grapes. They may have even made up the story in order to attract settlers.

Skraelings

In Vinland, the Viking settlers met Native Americans, who they called "Skraelings." At first, these were friendly meetings, as the Vikings traded milk for animal skins. However, fighting later broke out. The Vikings had better weapons, but they were outnumbered, so they abandoned their settlement.

Iceland

Floki Raven spent a cold winter in Iceland. He had failed to gather food for his livestock, so his animals starved to death. Disillusioned, he called the land "Iceland," which stuck. Despite the name, settlers soon began to arrive.

Bird's-eye view

In the 860s, Iceland was reached by Floki Raven, who carried ravens on board his ship to help with navigation. He would release each raven one by one. If a bird could not see land, it returned to the ship. Eventually, one raven saw land and flew away, with Floki's ship following.

Greenland

From Iceland, the Vikings sailed west, to another large, icy land. During the 980s, Erik the Red found an ice-free region on its west coast and established a settlement there. To encourage settlers, Erik called this land "Greenland."

Helluland

Leif Erikson, the son of Erik the Red, sailed from Greenland in around 1000 CE. During this voyage of exploration, he reached a low land, which resembled a single slab of rock. Leif named it Helluland (meaning "Slab land"). Sailing south, he came to a forested region he called Markland (meaning "Wood land").

Vinland

After two days of farther sailing, Leif reached a land with fine grazing and plenty of salmon. His men built houses and spent the winter there. They were delighted with the mild climate. They also found wild grapes, so Leif named it Vinland (meaning "Wine land"). Leif and his men had become the first Europeans to visit North America.

Travelers' tales

In the Middle Ages, long-distance travel was difficult and dangerous for Europeans trying to reach Asia or Africa. With only vague ideas of these distant lands, people loved hearing stories about the strange customs of foreigners. Some tales were written by genuine travelers, such as Friar John of Piano Carpini, the first European to reach Mongolia. Others, including stories of dog-headed men and gold-mining ants, were the wild inventions of the imagination.

John of Piano Carpini

Pope Innocent IV's ambassador was Friar John of Piano Carpini. He was about 65 years old and so overweight that he had trouble walking. Thanks to a number of horses supplied by the Mongols, he managed to travel 3,000 miles (4,800 km) in 106 days, arriving at the court of their new ruler Guyuk Khan.

Mongol Empire

By the 1240s, the Mongols had conquered a huge empire stretching from China to southern Russia. In 1241, their armies briefly invaded central Europe. Pope Innocent IV wanted to learn as much as possible about the Mongol threat. In 1245, he sent a mission to their court.

Genghis Khan

During the 1220s, Christians in Europe learned that their Muslim enemies in Asia were under attack from a powerful eastern king. People wondered if this was Prester John. In fact, it was Genghis Khan, ruler of the warlike Mongols from East Asia.

Prester John

One story told of a powerful Christian ruler named Prester John who lived somewhere in Asia or Africa. He was said to be so rich that his servants were kings in their own right. Europeans dreamed of finding him and winning his help in their wars.

Roll up, roll up!

oh no, I have vertigo!

Ready for the curtain call?

Smile nicely, Mongols

No photography, thank you

You don't scare me

Giddyup!

Get off!

Less pies for you, John

Armed and dangerous

King Khan

Khan I join you?

He rules

Hello, your highness

ENTRANCE

Welcome to my circus

Yippee!

Haven't seen you two in a while

oh, what a circus

Here's the slippery slope

Friar John's journey

The Mongols seemed savage and terrifying to Friar John. During his journey, he saw many signs of recent Mongol destruction, such as heaps of human bones, deserted towns, and ruined castles. Guyuk Khan told him that it was the Mongols' mission to rule the world.

William of Rubruck

In 1253, King Louis IX of France sent another friar, William of Rubruck, to see whether the Mongols could be converted to the Christian religion. Although William failed to convert them, he wrote a wonderful book describing Mongol customs, including their clothing, diet, and religious beliefs.

A guaranteed bestseller

Just a flying visit?

Dem bones, dem bones

There are no funny bones

What a load of baloney

Stop interrupting

Smelly foot

Sir John Mandeville

The most popular medieval travel book was *The Travels of Sir John Mandeville*, written in the 1350s. Its author claimed to be an English knight who had traveled across Asia. In reality, the stories were mostly made up or copied from earlier books.

Put your best foot forward

It's bigfoot

Giant foot folk

Inside Sir John Mandeville's book were descriptions of an island where the inhabitants each had one enormous foot. During the hottest part of the day, they would lie on their backs, using their giant feet as sunshades!

You look ruff

He's a bit mouthy

Tall story

Enough of your ant-ics

Gold-mining ants

According to Sir John Mandeville, Ceylon (modern-day Sri Lanka) was inhabited by ants as big as dogs. The ants spent their days mining for gold, which was found there in large quantities. This was a very old story, first told in the 5th century BCE by the ancient Greek writer Herodotus.

Island monsters

Sir John Mandeville wrote of islands off the coast of Asia that were home to dog-headed men and people without heads, who had eyes in each shoulder and mouths in the middle of their chests!

It's a minefield that way

15

Polo's passport

The Khan grew fond of Marco, who learned the Mongol language and told entertaining stories. As a reward, he gave Polo a gold passport, so that he could travel freely within his empire.

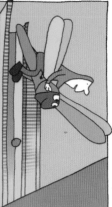

He looks like a fiery fellow

Do you hear something?

only the camel's stomach rumbling

Khan's Palace

After three years, the Polos reached Kublai Khan's palace in Khanbalik (modern-day Beijing). The walls were covered with gold and silver and decorated with pictures of dragons.

Gobi Desert

The Polos then crossed the massive Gobi Desert, a difficult journey that took them 30 days. The desert was said to be haunted, and at night strange voices could be heard.

Pamir Mountains

In central Asia, the Polos crossed the snowcapped Pamir Mountains, which stretch between Afghanistan and China. These are so high that they are nicknamed the "roof of the world."

Brrr...

Silk Road start

In 1271, 17-year-old Marco Polo set off with his father and uncle, both merchants who had visited China. They traveled on the Silk Road, the trade route between China and the West.

START

A slow start

This is just the beginning

Paper money

Polo was amazed to find that the Chinese used paper money, made from the bark of the mulberry tree. Paper was a Chinese invention. At the time, Europeans used metal coins.

Better check that your passport's valid

Money grows on trees

Can't buy me love

Dangerous animals

In addition to China, Polo visited Burma (Myanmar), Malaya, and India. He was surprised by the quantities of spices, such as pepper and ginger, grown there. He also saw dangerous animals, such as lions, tigers, and bears.

I can't bear having visitors

Asbestos and coal

In China, Polo saw a fire-resistant material, which he called "salamander" (asbestos). This was mined from mountains and spun into cloth. He also saw coal, which was not yet used as a fuel in Europe.

Express delivery

It's all mine!

Fantastic fuel

MARCO POLO

The most famous medieval European traveler was the Italian Marco Polo. After traveling east along the Silk Road, he reached the court of Kublai Khan, the Mongol ruler of China. Polo spent 17 years traveling around China and other parts of Asia. He returned to Europe after 24 years away and described the wonders that he had seen in a book. His reports of wealth in Asia inspired other explorers, such as Christopher Columbus, to find a way there.

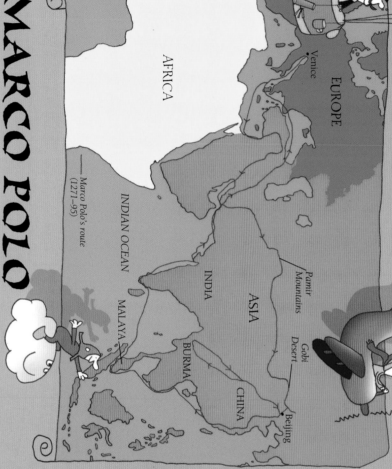

AFRICA

EUROPE

Venice

INDIAN OCEAN

ASIA

Pamir Mountains

Gobi Desert

Beijing

INDIA

CHINA

BURMA

MALAYA

— Marco Polo's route (1271–95)

Imperial Post

Polo was impressed by the efficiency of the Chinese Imperial Post. Along the roads of the Khan's empire were 10,000 posting stations with 200,000 horses, so that messengers could carry letters.

Taken prisoner

Back home in the Italian city of Venice, Polo joined a Venetian fleet fighting the Genoese in 1298. He was captured and imprisoned with a writer, Rustichello of Pisa, who recorded Polo's stories.

I got bored of listening

Good night, fellas

Tell us some more

Supreme storyteller

Thinking that Polo's stories were exaggerated, people asked him on his deathbed to admit that he was making things up. Polo replied that he hadn't even told half of everything he'd seen!

Really, Marco?

END

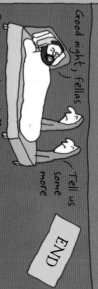

Shipwreck

While Battuta was at the port of Calicut, there was a terrible storm. His junk sank, with all the precious goods on board. He was scared to return to Delhi, where he might be punished for losing the Sultan's gifts.

My guts will be garters

It's going down a storm!

On to Calicut

A Muslim traveler rescued Battuta, helping him rejoin his companions. At the port of Calicut, the Sultan's gifts were loaded onto a Chinese junk.

Steady on, snakey.

Can I sit in the crow's nest?

Pirate attack

Leaving Sri Lanka, Battuta's ship almost sank during a storm. It was then attacked by 12 pirate ships. Once again, Battuta was robbed of everything except his pants, but was put ashore unharmed.

Great fit!

They're all the rage this season

What's all the fuss about my pants?

Paradise islands

Battuta then traveled to the Maldives and became a chief judge. After nine months, he moved on to Sri Lanka, where the king welcomed him.

This is the life

Attacked by Hindus

Battuta set off with the gifts from the Sultan for the Chinese emperor. Soon, Battuta became separated from his companions. He was captured by 40 Hindus, who robbed him of all his personal belongings, except his pants.

Red is my color

I hope they fit me!

They were my only pair

Judge and ambassador

Battuta reached Delhi, where the Sultan made him a *qadi* (judge) for three years. He was then sent to China as an ambassador, with gifts of horses, slaves, dancing girls, and fine cloths.

Party time!

Holy cities

When Battuta reached Mecca and Medina, he met Muslims from many lands. He heard that there were opportunities for Muslim scholars in India, and after a few years of travel, he set off.

It's a very popular haunt

Home at last

Battuta had many more adventures, including trips to China, Spain, and East and West Africa. In 1354, he returned home to Morocco, where he told his amazing travel stories to a scribe.

You Battuta believe it!

Strong start

In 1325, Ibn Battuta set off for Mecca and Medina. He traveled alone, riding on a donkey. For safety, he joined a caravan of fellow pilgrims. By the time the caravan reached Egypt, it was several thousand strong.

You're doing all the donkey work

Hyena heist

Crossing the Egyptian desert, Battuta's caravan encountered hyenas. Battuta stayed awake all night to chase them away. One hyena took a bag of dates from his bag and ran off with it!

Are they having a laugh?

Stop, thief!

As usual

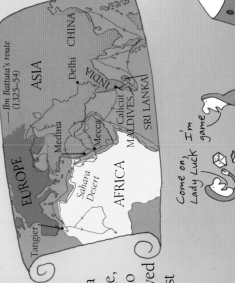

Ibn Battuta's route (1325–54)

EUROPE · ASIA · AFRICA · INDIA · CHINA · Tangier · Medina · Mecca · Delhi · Calicut · MALDIVES · SRI LANKA · Sahara Desert

Come on, Lady Luck, I'm game

IBN BATTUTA

The greatest traveler of the Middle Ages was Ibn Battuta, a Moroccan Muslim. It was the goal of every Muslim to visit the holy cities of Mecca and Medina in Arabia. After setting off on his pilgrimage, Battuta discovered that he loved traveling to new lands. For almost 30 years, he journeyed through Asia and Africa. He covered at least 75,000 miles (120,000 km), making an effort never to use the same road twice.

Chinese explorers

At various points in history, the Chinese set off on journeys of exploration—traveling overland to the West and by sea as far as East Africa. These journeys were exceptional events. The Chinese saw their homeland, called the "Middle Kingdom," as the center of the world, and they looked down on foreigners as savages. As a result, they usually had little interest in exploring other lands.

Zhang Qian

The earliest known Chinese explorer was Zhang Qian, who was sent by Emperor Wu to the rulers of central Asia in 138 BCE. After 13 years away, Qian returned home with stories of the amazing lands that he had visited.

The Silk Road

Zhang Qian's journey led to new trade links between China and the West, using a route called the "Silk Road." From China, merchants traveled west, carrying Chinese silks, which they traded for western products, such as grapes, walnuts, and flax.

Buddhist pilgrims

Following contact with the West, many Chinese people adopted a new religion called Buddhism. From the 4th century CE, Chinese Buddhist monks traveled to India to study their religion in its homeland. The earliest known Buddhist pilgrim was Fa Xian, who set off along the Silk Road in 399 CE.

Mighty Ming

Chinese power was at its peak under Emperor Yongle of the Ming dynasty, who ruled between 1402 and 1424. To increase Chinese influence, he sent out six huge naval expeditions to the western ocean, commanded by his admiral, Zheng He.

Chinese fleet

On his first voyage in 1405, Zheng He led a fleet of more than 200 ships, carrying around 27,000 men. The fleet included 62 great "treasure ships." The largest of these ships were approximately 400 ft (120 m) long and 160 ft (50 m) wide.

Spectacular seas

Back in China, Zheng He set up a tablet on which he wrote, "We have crossed immense water spaces and have seen in the ocean huge waves like mountains rising in the sky."

Map labels: ASIA, ARABIA, INDIA, THAILAND, AFRICA, INDIAN OCEAN, INDONESIA

— Voyages of Zheng He

Shipshape messages

The crewmembers of Zheng He's ships passed messages to each other using flags, lanterns, bells, carrier pigeons, gongs, and banners. As the ships arrived in distant lands, they must have presented a spectacular sight.

Spoon

Plate

Compass

Zheng He used a compass—a Chinese invention—to find his way. This was a spoon made of a magnetic mineral, and balanced on a plate. The spoon's changing position showed the direction the ship was traveling.

Great gifts

Zheng He's fleet visited Thailand, Indonesia, India, Arabia, and East Africa. He gave presents to local rulers, such as Ming vases, gold, silver, porcelain, and silk. In exchange, the rulers presented him with ivory, pearls, spices, and unusual animals and birds, including ostrich, lions, and zebras.

Junk sails

Chinese ships, called junks, had large sails that were stiffened with strips of bamboo. Unlike the square sails of European ships, these could be rotated at different angles, allowing a junk to sail into the wind.

Giraffe

The strangest animal Zheng He brought back to China was an East African giraffe, a gift for the emperor's private zoo.

That's the way

Just getting into the swing of things

What a cat-astrophe!

Meow for now

It's a motley crew

It's the golden age

We're sailing close to the wind

Blowin' in the wind

Not my usual neck of the woods

Two birds in the hand

So much junk

Wish this was a speedboat

I love junk food

Should I be looking more stern?

Don't chew with your mouth open

19

Henry the Navigator

The great European "Age of Exploration" was started in the 15th century by Prince Henry of Portugal, nicknamed "the Navigator." He was made governor of the southernmost part of Portugal in 1419 and sent out ships commanded by his household nobles to explore the Atlantic Ocean and the African coast. His court resembled a school for explorers, where new maps were made and scientists and sea captains exchanged ideas about navigation.

SAILING SCHOOL

Shiver his timbers

I wish he wood go away

Caravel

The Portuguese developed a new type of ship called a caravel. It had lateen (triangular) sails instead of square ones. This made it better at sailing into the wind, by "tacking" (sailing in a zigzag line).

It's plain sailing from now on

Winds

The prevailing wind off the coast of Portugal blows southwest, perfect for taking ships down the coast of Africa. Portuguese caravels could sail by the West African coast with the wind behind them and then return home by tacking against it.

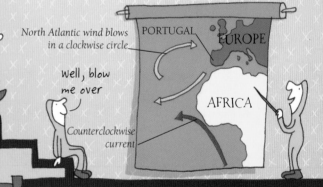

North Atlantic wind blows in a clockwise circle

PORTUGAL

EUROPE

Well, blow me over

AFRICA

Counterclockwise current

On the cape

At first, Prince Henry's sailors were scared of the unknown. Until 1434, they refused to pass a point called Cape Bojador, afraid that they would not be able to get home again.

Sew what?

Ripping yarn

Scaredy-cats

ENTRANCE

I'm not too cool for school

Hi, Henry

Cape Bojador

AFRICA

Here's where we fear to thread

Currents

As they sailed south, the Portuguese explorers learned about the Atlantic Ocean's water currents, as well as its winds. In the South Atlantic, the current flows in a giant counterclockwise circle, up the coast of Africa and then out to the west.

It's a current affair

Zacuto's tables

Astrolabe

In the 1470s, the Spanish astronomer Abraham Zacuto published tables showing the position of the Sun at different latitudes. Navigators measured the Sun's height with an astrolabe and then consulted Zacuto's tables to learn how far south or north they were.

Trading

Portuguese merchants were funding expeditions by the time of Henry's death in 1460. They traded with African chiefs, exchanging guns, cloth, salt, and metals for slaves, ivory, gold dust, and a spice called "guinea pepper."

What about guinea salt?

Got it

Slavery

The Portuguese began capturing Africans from their villages in the 1440s, bringing them back home to sell as slaves. This was the beginning of the European slave trade, which would last for the next 400 years.

Show me the money!

Yuck, the slimy world of finance

Bad news

The way to India

By the 1470s, the Portuguese goal was to find the way to India, with its rich spice markets. Hopes were raised when explorers found the Guinea coast swinging sharply east. Unfortunately, they were still only halfway down the African coast.

Take me to India

And the winner is...

The suspense is killing me

START

RACE TO INDIA

Guinea gold

Look at these amateurs!

Between 1469–74, voyages were sponsored by a rich merchant named Fernão Gomes. His ships explored the Guinea coast, where they found rich sources of gold.

Go-mes! Go-mes!

Diogo Cao

In the 1480s, the explorer Diogo Cao made two voyages, discovering another 1,490 miles (2,400 km) of coastline. It was now clear that Africa was much bigger than anyone had previously suspected.

Inscribed stone crosses were left by Cao to mark his discoveries

Cao-me on!

Cape of Good Hope

Bart the bolt!

The southern tip of Africa was finally rounded in 1488 by Bartolomeu Dias. He named it the "Cape of Storms" after the weather that he encountered there, but King John II did not like this name and renamed it the "Cape of Good Hope." At last, the way to India was open.

On to India

Following Bartolomeu Dias's rounding of South Africa, the route to India opened up. In 1497, King Manuel I of Portugal decided to send an expedition there, led by a young nobleman named Vasco da Gama. King Manuel hoped that da Gama would return with valuable spices, as well as news of Christian rulers said to be living in India. On July 8 of that year, da Gama set off on his great voyage, with four ships and 170 men.

Sturdy ships

Two of da Gama's ships were specially built for the voyage. These were not caravels but larger ships, called carracks. Unlike caravals, carracks had square sails, which would prove easier to handle in the rough weather of the South Atlantic.

FILM STUDIO ENTRANCE

No aliens allowed

Another day, another dollar

CATERING VAN

Nice as pie

Sorry, only meat

Tofu burger?

Weighty goods

The ships were loaded with enough supplies for a three-year voyage. There were casks of wine, salted beef and pork, and weapons and ammunition. Trade goods, to exchange for Indian spices, included jars of honey, woolen hats, and coral beads.

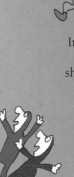

Into the Atlantic

Instead of following the coast of Africa, like previous explorers had done, the ships sailed southwest, and out into the ocean. Da Gama was using the wind system of the South Atlantic, which blows in a counterclockwise circle. He would have the wind blowing behind him during his journey.

This should put us on the map

Gale force, please

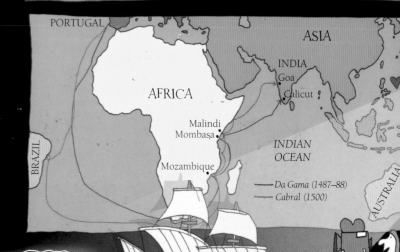

SILENCE ON SET: FILMING IN PROGRESS

PORTUGAL

AFRICA

ASIA

INDIA
Goa
Calicut

Malindi
Mombasa

BRAZIL

Mozambique

INDIAN OCEAN

AUSTRALIA

— Da Gama (1487–88)
— Cabral (1500)

Oh my cod

Aaar! You can't stay in there all day

Land at last!

Da Gama's ships spent 13 weeks out of sight of land. When the explorers finally saw the coast of Africa, in November 1497, they celebrated by decorating their ships with flags, firing guns, and putting on their best clothes.

Get your glad rags on

Yikes!

Watch where you point that

You must be a runner

22

Who took the sail?

Wood you believe it?

Carracking boat!

Accidental find

Da Gama's voyage was quickly followed up. In 1500, fellow Portugese navigator Pedro Cabral sailed to India with a fleet of 13 well-armed ships. On the way, he accidentally discovered Brazil and claimed it for Portugal. Cabral returned with ships loaded with spices and rubies.

—No

Will they invite me to the premiere?

Pedro leads the life!

A box office smash

Return journey

On his return journey, da Gama made the mistake of sailing against the monsoon wind. Crossing the Indian Ocean took four months, and almost half his men died from scurvy, caused by lack of fresh food. In September of 1499, he returned to Portugal, with his ships loaded with spices.

Saint Shiva

The Portuguese had never seen Hindus before. They were amazed by their colorful temples, with statues of strange-looking gods, such as Shiva. Da Gama knew that Muslims and Jews did not worship statues. He mistakenly thought that the Indian people were Christians and that Shiva was a Christian saint.

Wait up!

Trade port

On May 20, 1498, the fleet reached Calicut, a busy port on the Indian coast. The wealthy ruler, the Samorin, was not impressed by the Portuguese, who had brought no expensive gifts for him. Despite this, he allowed them to trade.

Slow down

Less haste, more speed

What goodies do you have for me?

What a terrible noise

Take 267

This is your pilot speaking

Action!

New navigator

In Malindi, da Gama was lucky to hire an Arab pilot, who offered to show him the way to India. This meant sailing with the seasonal monsoon wind, which blows to the northeast in the summer and changes direction in the winter.

Unwelcome visitor

Da Gama sailed on into the Indian Ocean, where no European ships had gone before. In East Africa, he visited three Muslim ports— Mozambique, Mombasa, and Malindi. Local rulers did not welcome Christians, nor their trade goods.

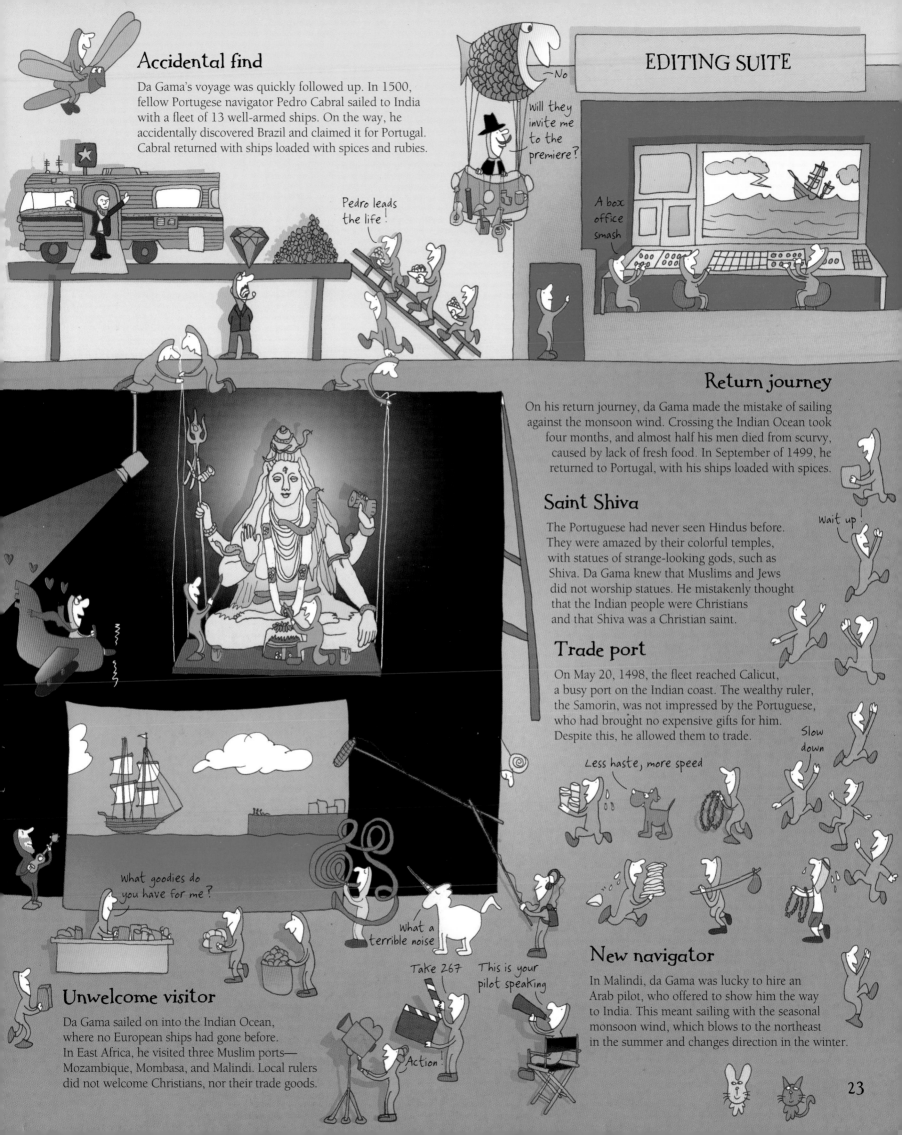

Sailing west

Christopher Columbus was an Italian seafarer, who had read about the wealth of Asia from Marco Polo's book. Columbus believed that the quickest sea route was not south around Africa, but west across the Atlantic Ocean, thinking Asia to be on the other side. He was wrong, but his voyages led to the discovery of a great continent between Europe and Asia, later called America.

Searching for a sponsor

After being turned down by the Portuguese king in 1484, Columbus moved to Spain. He promised King Ferdinand and Queen Isabella that his voyage would make them rich and spread the Christian faith to Asia. In 1492, they agreed to sponsor his plans, and Columbus started his preparations.

Setting sail

On August 3, 1492, Columbus set sail with 90 men on board three ships—the *Santa Maria*, *Pinta*, and *Niña*. They sailed southwest to the Canary Islands, since Columbus believed that Japan was located west of this point. He knew that the winds there usually blew to the west and would therefore help them across.

You need to cool off

All aboard the Colum-bus!

Water way to paint!

Dead reckoning

Columbus navigated by "dead reckoning"—keeping track of his ship's direction and the distance that it had traveled. To calculate the distance, Columbus had to keep a record of the speed of his ship over a set period of time.

Magnetic compass points north

Sargasso Sea

On September 16, the ships found themselves sailing through a mass of bright green seaweed, covered with crabs. The sailors were excited by this, thinking that land was near. In fact, they had discovered the Sargasso Sea, a giant area of floating seaweed in the middle of the Atlantic Ocean.

All I sea are weeds!

Near mutiny

As they sailed farther away from land, the men grew increasingly worried. On October 10, the crew of the *Santa Maria* demanded that Columbus give up his foolish plan and take them home, but he refused to give in to their demands.

He's making a show of us!

Don't go!

Boo hiss!

Right direction
To find his direction, Columbus used a magnetic compass.

Hourglass
He measured time using an hourglass, which he turned over every half hour.

Speed
To estimate their speed, he threw chips of wood over the side, seeing how fast the ship passed them.

Chart
At regular intervals, Columbus marked the course he had traveled on a chart.

Don't be so crabby

They're staging a protest!

Land ahoy!

At last, land was sighted on October 12. Columbus had reached the Bahamas. Going ashore, he was welcomed by astonished but friendly people. Thinking that he had reached the Indies (Asia), Columbus mistakenly called them "Indians." As a result of this error, Native Americans are still sometimes called Indians today.

Islands explored

Columbus sailed on, exploring the coasts of Cuba and Haiti, which he called "Hispaniola" (the Spanish island). He thought that Hispaniola would be the perfect place for a Spanish settlement. Nothing Columbus saw matched Marco Polo's descriptions of Asia, but he was still certain that Japan was nearby.

Homecoming

Columbus returned to Spain in March 1493, bringing captured natives, colorful parrots, and strange foods, including corn and pineapples. The delighted monarchs rewarded him with the title "Admiral of the Ocean Sea." They asked him to lead a new expedition to found a Spanish colony in Hispaniola.

Voyaging on

Columbus made three more voyages, exploring the coasts of the South and Central American mainland. He decided that he must have reached the "Earthly paradise," described in the Bible.

The voyages of Christopher Columbus

- 1st voyage (1492–93)
- 2nd voyage (1493–96)
- 3rd voyage (1498–1500)
- 4th voyage (1502–04)

NORTH AMERICA
NEWFOUNDLAND
ATLANTIC OCEAN
EUROPE
BAHAMAS
CUBA
HISPANIOLA
AFRICA
SOUTH AMERICA

John Cabot

Soon, other explorers were crossing the Atlantic Ocean. In 1497, John Cabot, an Italian sailor living in England, made a northern crossing and reached Newfoundland. Like Columbus, he believed that he was in Asia.

A new world

An Italian named Amerigo Vespucci explored the mainland in 1499 and 1501. He argued that it was not part of Asia but a "new world." The mapmaker Martin Waldseemuller suggested naming it "America" in his honor, and it has stuck to this day.

AROUND THE WORLD

Like Christopher Columbus before him, Portuguese nobleman Ferdinand Magellan believed that a western route to Asia would be quicker than the eastern one used by the Portuguese. He needed to find a passage of water through America, but mistakenly assumed that Asia must only be a short distance farther. Although Magellan did not complete his journey, the expedition that he commanded resulted in the very first voyage around the world.

Setting off

Magellan's first voyages were to Asia and for the king of Portugal. When Magellan moved to Spain, he won backing for his western-route plan from King Charles I. On September 20, 1519, he set off with a fleet of five ships, carrying around 265 men, including the Spaniard Juan Sebastián Elcano.

In South America

After sailing down the side of South America, Magellan spent the winter on the coast. His Spanish captains disliked taking orders from a foreigner, so they mutinied (rebelled). In punishment, Magellan had one captain executed and two others marooned (left behind).

Big Foot Land

Magellan named the southernmost part of South America *Patagonia* ("Big Foot land"), after the tall native Americans that he saw living there. One of his ships was wrecked in Patagonia, though its crew was rescued.

Sailing through the strait

In October of 1520, Magellan finally found a strait (passage of water) through South America. One ship deserted the expedition and sailed back to Spain, leaving Magellan with only three. It took them a difficult 38 days to sail through the strait, which was later named after him.

World's first

On reaching Spain, on September 6, 1522, after his three-year voyage, Elcano had completed the first journey around the world. King Charles V awarded him a coat of arms. It was a globe with the motto, "You went around me first."

Returning home

On their homeward journey, *Trinidad* was left behind due to damage caused during the voyage. Only *Victoria* returned to Spain, with just 18 survivors, and all of them sick with scurvy. Yet the ship's cargo of cloves meant that the expedition had still made an excellent profit.

The Spice Islands

With too few men to crew their three remaining ships, one was abandoned. Under a new commander, Juan Sebastián Elcano, the two ships, called *Trinidad* and *Victoria*, sailed on to the Moluccas (Spice Islands). There they loaded up with cloves and other spices.

Fatal Philippines

In March of 1521, Magellan finally reached the Philippines, where he and his men were involved in a local war. During a battle on Mactan Island, the locals attacked them with swords and bamboo spears. Magellan and several of his men were killed.

Pacific crossing

Magellan's ships spent four months in the open sea. Food supplies ran low, and the men grew sick with scurvy, due to a lack of vitamin C. They were so hungry that they ate leather and sawdust and rats were sold for gold coins.

Peaceful Ocean

After the strait, the expedition then sailed into an ocean. Impressed by the sea's calmness, Magellan named it the *Mar Pacifico* (Peaceful Ocean). He expected to reach the Indies in a short time. In fact, he had entered the world's largest ocean, which covers one third of the planet's surface.

SPANISH CONQUISTADORS

In the early 16th century, Spanish explorers learned that the American mainland was home to wealthy civilizations, rich in gold and silver. The two great empires were the Aztecs in Mexico and the Incas in Peru. The Spaniards set out to conquer these peoples, with the advantage of guns, horses, steel swords, and armor. Although there were greater numbers of Aztecs and Incas, they only had stone-bladed weapons.

Montezuma II

The Aztec ruler, Montezuma II, heard that strange, metal-wearing beings had arrived on the coast. He did not know if they were gods or men. Too scared to attack the Spaniards, Montezuma sent presents to Cortés.

In Tenochtitlan

Cortés marched to Tenochtitlan, forging alliances with Mexican peoples who hated their Aztec rulers. Although Montezuma II welcomed Cortés, the Spaniards then took the emperor prisoner, using him to give their orders to the Aztecs.

Final conquest

In May of 1520, the Aztecs rose up against the Spanish and drove them out of Tenochtitlan. However, Cortés gathered a new army from Cuba and, helped by his Mexican allies, returned to conquer the city three months later.

Sacrifice

The Aztecs would occasionally use a prisoner as a ritual sacrifice to their gods. During battle, they did not try to kill their enemies, but instead to capture them alive. This would prove a disadvantage when fighting against the Spanish.

Ready to conquer

In 1519, Hernándo Cortés, a Spanish settler in Cuba, led an expedition of 11 ships with around 500 men to the coast of Mexico. He realized that he had discovered a wealthy empire and resolved to conquer it.

The Aztecs

The empire of this warlike people stretched all the way from the Pacific Ocean to the Gulf of Mexico. Their capital, Tenochtitlan, was dominated by tall pyramid-shaped temples, where prisoners were offered as sacrifices to the Aztec gods.

NORTH AMERICA

GULF OF MEXICO

CUBA

CARIBBEAN SEA

Tenochtitlan

Aztec Empire

Hernándo Cortés's route to Tenochtitlan (1519)

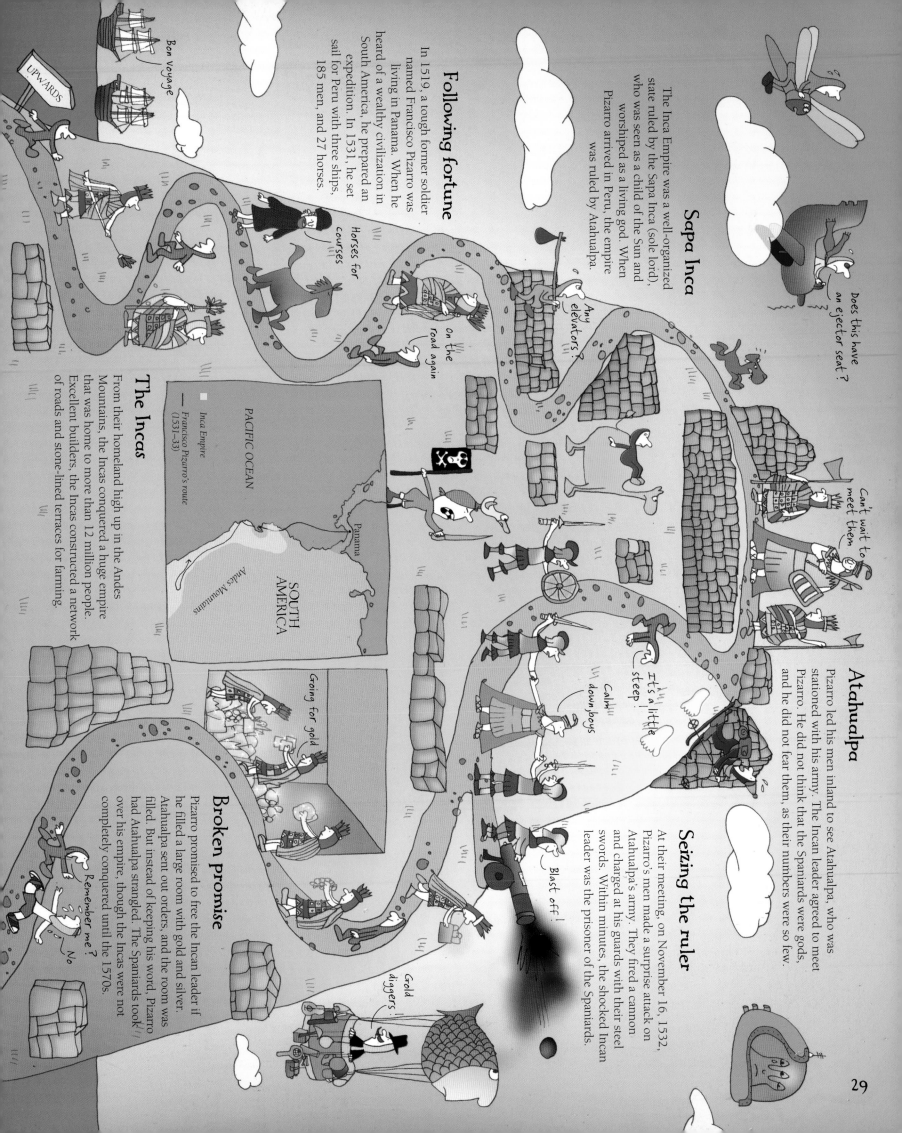

Sapa Inca

The Inca Empire was a well-organized state ruled by the Sapa Inca (sole lord), who was seen as a child of the Sun and worshiped as a living god. When Pizarro arrived in Peru, the empire was ruled by Atahualpa.

Following fortune

In 1519, a tough former soldier named Francisco Pizarro was living in Panama. When he heard of a wealthy civilization in South America, he prepared an expedition. In 1531, he set sail for Peru with three ships, 185 men, and 27 horses.

The Incas

From their homeland high up in the Andes Mountains, the Incas conquered a huge empire that was home to more than 12 million people. Excellent builders, the Incas constructed a network of roads and stone-lined terraces for farming.

Atahualpa

Pizarro led his men inland to see Atahualpa, who was stationed with his army. The Incan leader agreed to meet Pizarro. He did not think that the Spaniards were gods, and he did not fear them, as their numbers were so few.

Seizing the ruler

At their meeting, on November 16, 1532, Pizarro's men made a surprise attack on Atahualpa's army. They fired a cannon and charged at his guards with their steel swords. Within minutes, the shocked Incan leader was the prisoner of the Spaniards.

Broken promise

Pizarro promised to free the Incan leader if he filled a large room with gold and silver. Atahualpa sent out orders, and the room was filled. But instead of keeping his word, Pizarro had Atahualpa strangled. The Spaniards took over his empire, though the Incas were not completely conquered until the 1570s.

PACIFIC OCEAN

SOUTH AMERICA

Panama

Andes Mountains

— Francisco Pizarro's route (1531–33)

■ Inca Empire

UPWARDS

Bon voyage

Horses for courses

On the road again

Any elevators?

Can't wait to meet them

Does this have an ejector seat?

It's a little steep!

Calm down boys

Blast off!

Going for gold

Remember me?

No

Gold diggers!

29

OLD AND NEW WORLDS

Before 1492, there had been virtually no contact between the "Old World" (Eurasia and Africa) and the "New World" (the Americas). Each had its own distinctive animals, ideas, and technologies. Following Christopher Columbus's voyage across the Atlantic Ocean in 1492, the two worlds were brought together. This "Columbian Exchange" involved people, animals, ideas, and diseases crossing between the two worlds in both directions, and it changed the lives of everyone.

Diseases

European settlers brought many new diseases to the Americas, including smallpox, influenza, measles, chickenpox, and typhus. Native Americans, who had no resistance to these diseases, died in huge numbers. As the diseases spread, around 80 percent of the native population was wiped out.

African slaves

So many Native Americans died from new diseases that the European conquerors did not have enough people to work on their lands. From the 16th to the 19th centuries, around ten million African slaves were shipped over to the Americas.

Food

Across the world, people benefited from new food plants. The New World received wheat, oats, barley, coffee, tea, sugar, rice, and onions. Meanwhile, the Old World gained corn, potatoes, tomatoes, chili peppers, pineapples, peanuts, and chocolate.

Pesky pests

Unintentionally transported in the holds of ships, pests passed in both directions between the Old and New Worlds. Brown rats and cockroaches, which spread many diseases, moved from Europe to the Americas. The North American Colorado Beetle can wipe out entire potato crops, and in the 19th century it spread across most of Europe and Asia.

Manioc

One of the most useful discoveries was the food plant manioc, also known as cassava, found by Christopher Columbus in South America. Manioc resists drought and pests and grows well, even in bad soil. It is now eaten in tropical regions, from Africa to Southeast Asia.

OLD WORLD MARKET

NEW WORLD MARKET

This is a little old hat

DISEASE KIOSK

Highly contagious

A whole new world ....

Where's my sickbed?

I need to lie down

Did I catch something?

You look like I feel

You're such a nuisance

Takes one to know one!

We must stop meeting like this!

Move over, ratbag

You shouldn't have!

Spoiled for choice

There goes the diet

FABULOUS FOOD!

You manioc!

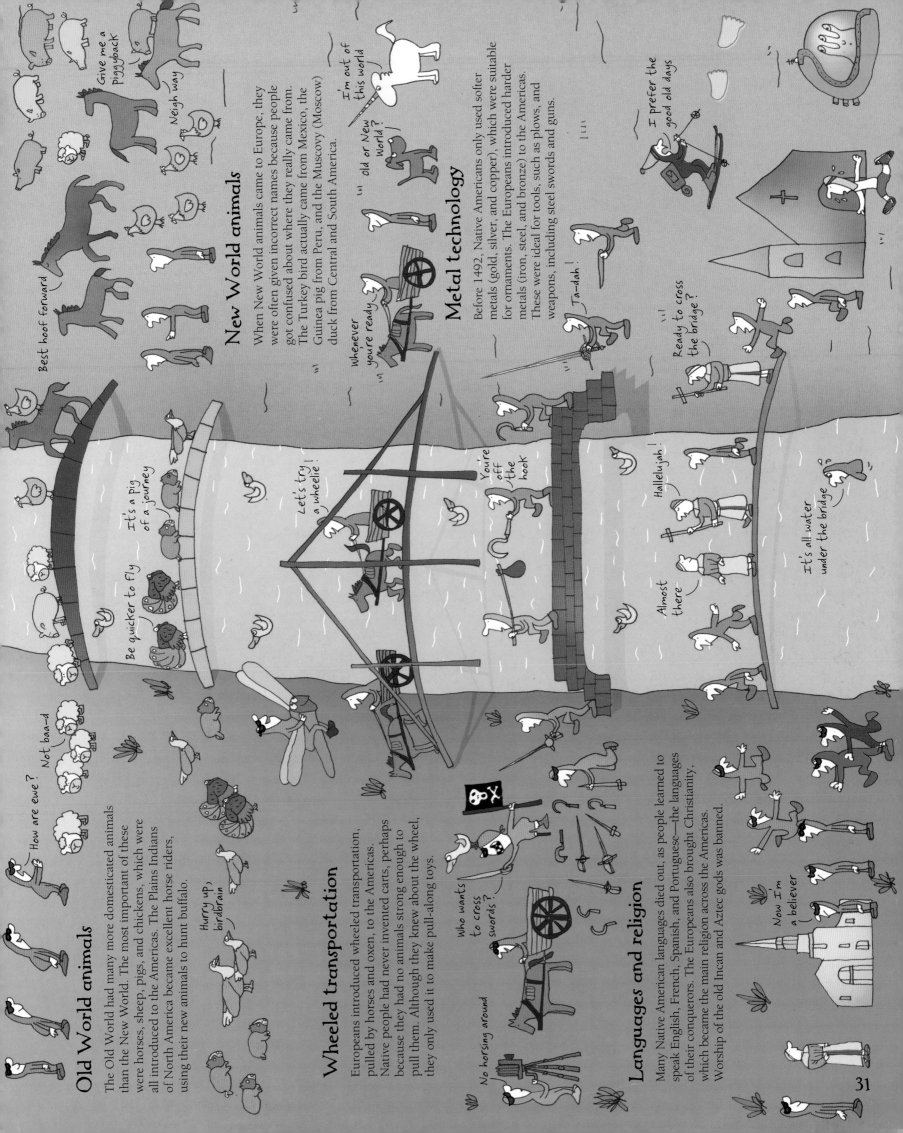

Old World animals

The Old World had many more domesticated animals than the New World. The most important of these were horses, sheep, pigs, and chickens, which were all introduced to the Americas. The Plains Indians of North America became excellent horse riders, using their new animals to hunt buffalo.

Wheeled transportation

Europeans introduced wheeled transportation, pulled by horses and oxen, to the Americas. Native people had never invented carts, perhaps because they had no animals strong enough to pull them. Although they knew about the wheel, they only used it to make pull-along toys.

Languages and religion

Many Native American languages died out, as people learned to speak English, French, Spanish, and Portuguese—the languages of their conquerors. The Europeans also brought Christianity, which became the main religion across the Americas. Worship of the old Incan and Aztec gods was banned.

New World animals

When New World animals came to Europe, they were often given incorrect names because people got confused about where they really came from. The Turkey bird actually came from Mexico, the Guinea pig from Peru, and the Muscovy (Moscow) duck from Central and South America.

Metal technology

Before 1492, Native Americans only used softer metals (gold, silver, and copper), which were suitable for ornaments. The Europeans introduced harder metals (iron, steel, and bronze) to the Americas. These were ideal for tools, such as plows, and weapons, including steel swords and guns.

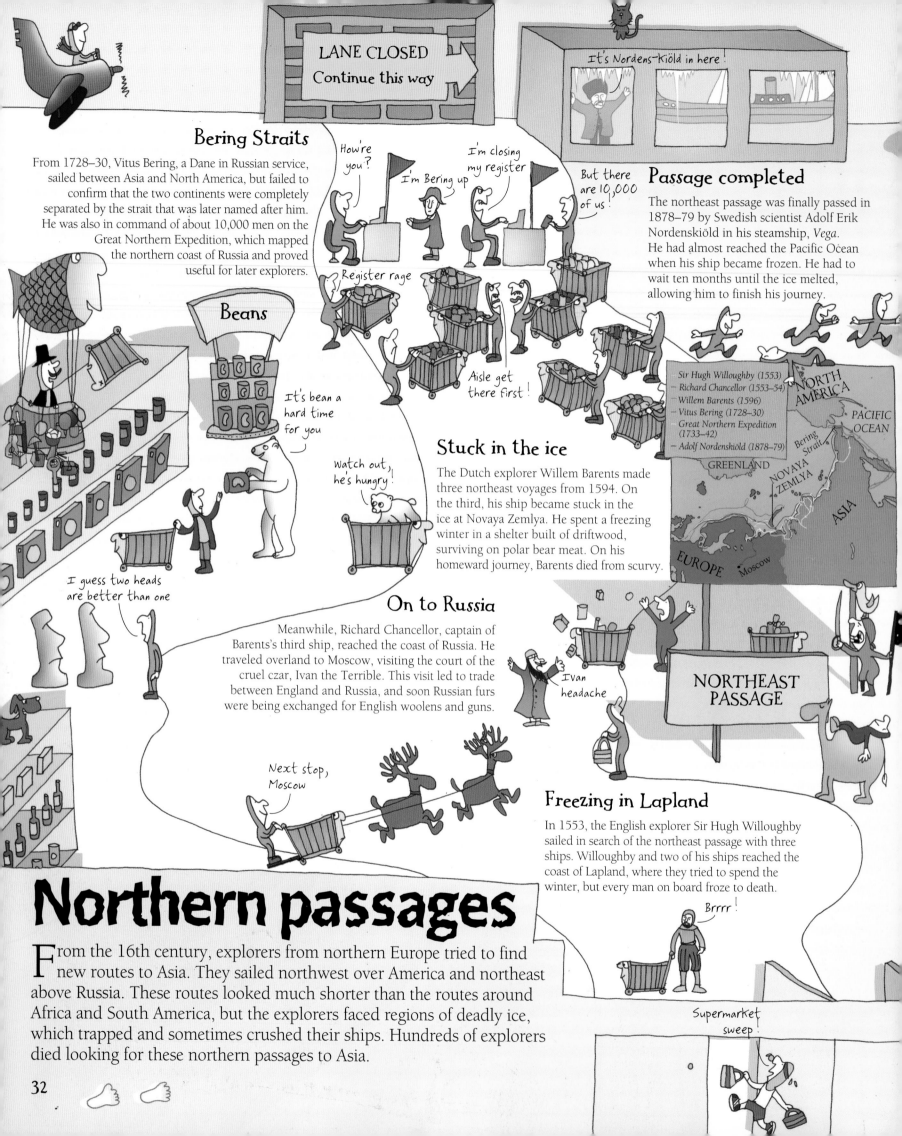

LANE CLOSED
Continue this way

It's Nordens-Kiöld in here!

Bering Straits

From 1728–30, Vitus Bering, a Dane in Russian service, sailed between Asia and North America, but failed to confirm that the two continents were completely separated by the strait that was later named after him. He was also in command of about 10,000 men on the Great Northern Expedition, which mapped the northern coast of Russia and proved useful for later explorers.

How're you?

I'm Bering up

I'm closing my register

But there are 10,000 of us!

Register rage

Passage completed

The northeast passage was finally passed in 1878–79 by Swedish scientist Adolf Erik Nordenskiöld in his steamship, *Vega*. He had almost reached the Pacific Ocean when his ship became frozen. He had to wait ten months until the ice melted, allowing him to finish his journey.

Beans

It's bean a hard time for you

Watch out, he's hungry!

Aisle get there first!

Stuck in the ice

The Dutch explorer Willem Barents made three northeast voyages from 1594. On the third, his ship became stuck in the ice at Novaya Zemlya. He spent a freezing winter in a shelter built of driftwood, surviving on polar bear meat. On his homeward journey, Barents died from scurvy.

Sir Hugh Willoughby (1553)
– Richard Chancellor (1553–54)
– Willem Barents (1596)
– Vitus Bering (1728–30)
– Great Northern Expedition (1733–42)
– Adolf Nordenskiöld (1878–79)

NORTH AMERICA
PACIFIC OCEAN
Bering Strait
GREENLAND
NOVAYA ZEMLYA
ASIA
EUROPE · Moscow

I guess two heads are better than one

On to Russia

Meanwhile, Richard Chancellor, captain of Barents's third ship, reached the coast of Russia. He traveled overland to Moscow, visiting the court of the cruel czar, Ivan the Terrible. This visit led to trade between England and Russia, and soon Russian furs were being exchanged for English woolens and guns.

Ivan headache

NORTHEAST PASSAGE

Next stop, Moscow

Freezing in Lapland

In 1553, the English explorer Sir Hugh Willoughby sailed in search of the northeast passage with three ships. Willoughby and two of his ships reached the coast of Lapland, where they tried to spend the winter, but every man on board froze to death.

Brrrr!

Northern passages

From the 16th century, explorers from northern Europe tried to find new routes to Asia. They sailed northwest over America and northeast above Russia. These routes looked much shorter than the routes around Africa and South America, but the explorers faced regions of deadly ice, which trapped and sometimes crushed their ships. Hundreds of explorers died looking for these northern passages to Asia.

Supermarket sweep

Fool's gold

One of the first attempts to find a northwest passage was made by the Englishman Martin Frobisher, who made three voyages in the 1570s. He brought some Inuit (Eskimo peoples) back to England, along with a few worthless yellow rocks he thought to be gold.

Lost at sea

Henry Hudson sailed into the Canadian Arctic in 1610 and discovered a large sea, later named the Hudson Bay. After a winter trapped in the ice, his crew mutinied and cast him adrift in a small boat with his son and seven sick crewmen. They were never seen again.

Arctic disaster

The British Navy sent Sir John Franklin to find the passage in 1845. He commanded two well-equipped ships, with enough food supplies for three years. Franklin and his crew of 128 men were never seen alive by Europeans again. This was the worst disaster in Arctic exploration.

Tragic tale

From 1848 onward, around 40 expeditions searched for Sir Franklin, mapping the Canadian Arctic in the process. They learned from a note and from Inuit accounts that Franklin's ships had been trapped and then crushed by ice. All the men eventually died of starvation and sickness while trying to escape overland.

Sailor's goal

Although the northwest passage was of no practical use, completing it had now become a goal for explorers. It was finally sailed through in 1903–06 by Norwegian explorer Roald Amundsen, in a converted herring boat named *Gjoa*. His success was due to his use of Inuit survival methods.

33

CROSSING NORTH AMERICA

From the 16th century, the North American continent was explored in the south by the Spanish and in the north and west by the British and French. The Spanish were looking for gold, but they only found hostile regions of deserts and mountains. Meanwhile, the British and French were searching for a waterway to the Pacific Ocean. Instead, they encountered a fertile land of rivers and lakes, rich in beaver and salmon, but home to fierce grizzly bears.

Seven cities of gold

In Mexico, the Spanish heard rumors of seven rich cities of gold somewhere in North America. In 1540, Francisco de Coronado headed a large expedition in search of these cities. He reached the Great Plains and saw herds of buffalo (bison), but found no gold.

Bark canoes

French and British explorers traveled in Native American canoes built from birch bark. These were easy to repair and light enough to be carried overland from river to river.

Map legend:
— Hernando de Soto (1539–43)
— Francisco de Coronado (1540–42)
— Samuel de Champlain (1608–16)
— Robert de la Salle (1679–82)
— Alexander Mackenzie (1789)
— Alexander Mackenzie (1792–93)
— Meriwether Lewis and William Clark (1804–05)

Samuel de Champlain

The greatest French explorer was Samuel de Champlain, who founded the settlement of Quebec on the Saint Lawrence River in 1608. He was the first European to explore the Great Lakes, from 1609 onward. One of these was later named Lake Champlain, in his honor.

Swamped in Florida

In 1539, Spanish explorer Hernando de Soto crossed into America from Cuba with an army of 622 men. He struggled though the Florida swamps and fought battles with native Americans in pursuit of gold. When he reached the Mississippi River, he died of a fever. There was no gold to be found.

Louisiana

Another Frenchman, Robert de la Salle, traveled south from the Great Lakes in 1682. He followed the great Mississippi River all the way to the Gulf of Mexico and claimed the entire Mississippi region for France, naming it Louisiana after King Louis XIV.

Over the Rockies

Alexander Mackenzie reached the Pacific Ocean on his second attempt in 1793 by following a series of rivers. This made him the first white man to cross America north of Mexico. He had to traverse the snowy Rocky Mountains, which formed a great barrier, blocking travel to the coast.

Snowshoes

Explorers learned from native American guides how to live and travel in the wild. They adopted the locals' webbed snowshoes made of wood and leather, which stopped them sinking into the soft snow.

Lewis and Clarke

In 1776, Britain's American colonies became the new United States of America. In 1804, U.S. President Thomas Jefferson sent two explorers, Meriwether Lewis and William Clark, on an expedition to follow the course of the great Missouri River. He hoped that it would lead to the Pacific.

Fur traders

The northern lakes and rivers were rich in beaver. The soft, dense, and waterproof fur was prized in Europe, where it was made into hats. Canadian exploration was mostly carried out by two rival fur-trading companies, the Hudson's Bay Company and the Northwest Company.

River of Disappointment

The Scottish fur trader Alexander Mackenzie traced the course of a great western Canadian river in 1789, hoping that it led to the Pacific Ocean. When he found that it took him north to the Arctic, he named it the "River of Disappointment." It was later called the Mackenzie River.

Native helper

After crossing the Rocky Mountains, Lewis and Clark reached the Pacific Ocean in November 1805. They were guided by a Native American woman named Sacagawea, who had a baby during the journey.

Hunting

Native American hunters supplied the explorers with food, including deer and salmon. They fished with spears and basket traps and shot deer and bear using guns, supplied by the fur traders.

Charting the Pacific

The greatest Pacific explorers were the ancient Polynesians, whose ancestors came from Southeast Asia. They traveled around the Pacific Ocean, looking for new island homes. By the 11th century CE, they had settled a huge area, from Hawaii in the north, to New Zealand in the southwest, and Easter Island in the southeast. When European explorers discovered their widely scattered islands in the 18th century, they were amazed to find them inhabited by a single people.

— Routes taken by the Polynesians

ASIA
NORTH AMERICA
PACIFIC OCEAN
HAWAIIAN ISLANDS
AUSTRALIA
NEW ZEALAND
EASTER ISLAND

We're making an exhibition of ourselves

Great voyages

At a time when European ships rarely sailed out of sight of land, Polynesians were making voyages in open sea of up to 3,000 miles (4,800 km). They sailed in large, open-decked canoes, of around 98 ft (30 m) in length, with twin hulls tied side by side. They navigated using the position of the Sun and the stars.

Beginners welcome

ART STUDIO

I come from a land down under

Polynesian planning

Voyages were carefully planned to find new islands to settle. One double canoe could carry around 50 people, as well as pigs, chickens, and dogs. They also brought many different plant seedlings, such as sweet potatoes and breadfruit. Rats also traveled with them, either as stowaways on board or as emergency food supplies.

Copy my sense of perspective

I prefer a more abstract approach

Get my best angle

Art boars me

No use crying over spilled paint

I've drawn a blank

I'm world-renowned

Unknown continent

During the 18th century, Europeans searched the Pacific Ocean for a southern continent. Since the time of the ancient Greeks, people had imagined that a land existed to balance the continents of the northern half of the globe. On maps, it was shown as "Terra Australis Incognita" (Unknown Southern land).

36

Hawaii

Captain Cook discovered the Hawaiian Islands in 1778, where he watched the locals surfing on wooden boards. He was amazed that they spoke the same language as the Tahitians, who lived 2,600 miles (4,200 km) away. Cook wrote, "How shall we account for this nation's spreading so far over this vast ocean?"

Death in Hawaii

When he first arrived in Hawaii, Captain Cook was treated as a god. However, on his second visit in 1779, he outstayed his welcome. One of his small boats was stolen, so Cook went ashore to try and get it back. A fight broke out with the locals, and he was killed.

ASIA

NORTH AMERICA

Cook's first voyage (1768–71)

Cook's second voyage (1772–75)

Cook's third voyage (1776–79)

PACIFIC OCEAN

SOUTH AMERICA

TAHITI

AUSTRALASIA

NEW ZEALAND

ANTARCTICA

Captain Cook

The greatest explorer of the Pacific Ocean was British Captain James Cook, who made three great voyages between 1768 and 1779. Among his many discoveries, he mapped the coasts of New Zealand and the east coast of Australia and proved that there was no great southern continent.

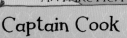

Easter Island

Dutch explorer Jacob Roggeveen found the most eastern Polynesian settlement in 1722. He called it Easter Island after his arrival date. He reported that the local islanders worshiped huge stone statues.

Tahiti

In 1767, British explorer Samuel Wallis became the first European to visit Tahiti. The following year, a French expedition arrived. One of the French sailors was a woman disguised as a man. Her name was Jeanne Baré, and she was the first woman to sail around the world.

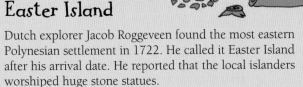

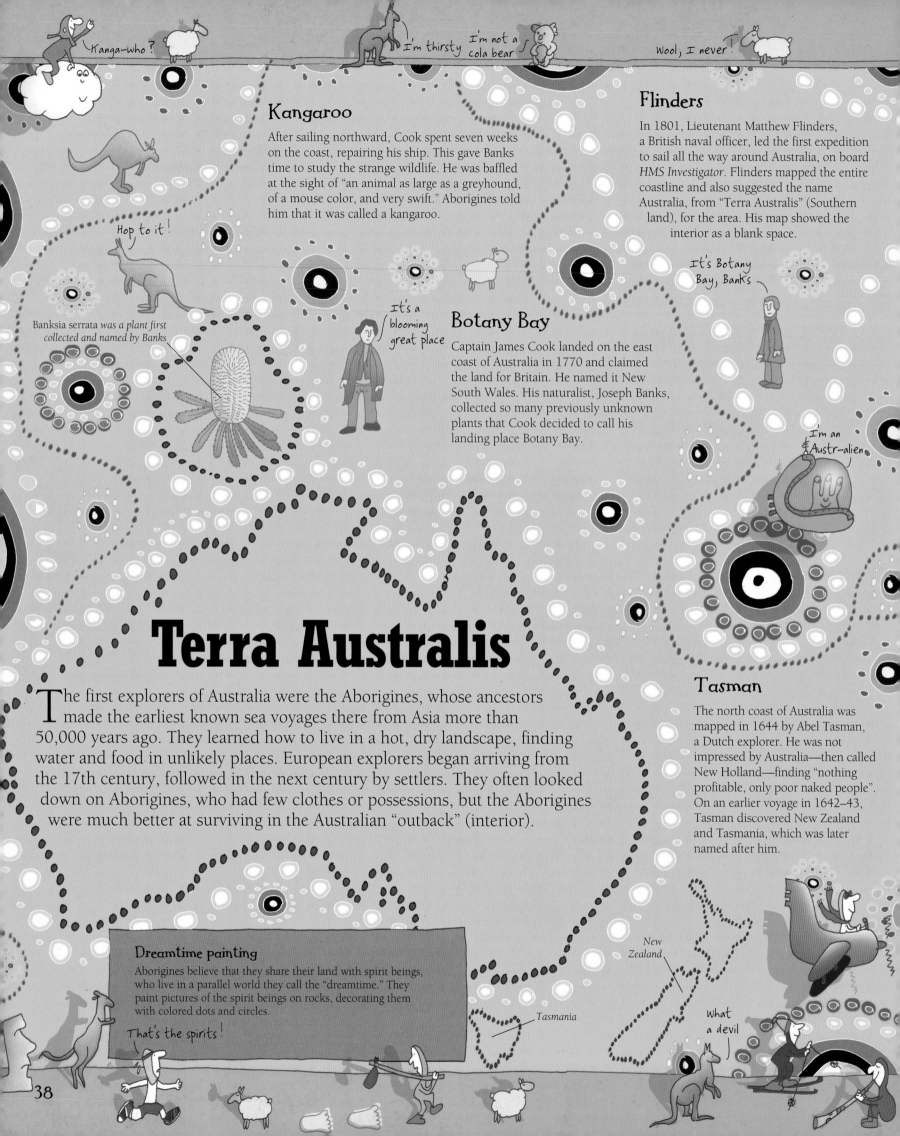

Kangaroo

After sailing northward, Cook spent seven weeks on the coast, repairing his ship. This gave Banks time to study the strange wildlife. He was baffled at the sight of "an animal as large as a greyhound, of a mouse color, and very swift." Aborigines told him that it was called a kangaroo.

Flinders

In 1801, Lieutenant Matthew Flinders, a British naval officer, led the first expedition to sail all the way around Australia, on board *HMS Investigator*. Flinders mapped the entire coastline and also suggested the name Australia, from "Terra Australis" (Southern land), for the area. His map showed the interior as a blank space.

Hop to it!

It's Botany Bay, Banks

Banksia serrata was a plant first collected and named by Banks

It's a blooming great place

Botany Bay

Captain James Cook landed on the east coast of Australia in 1770 and claimed the land for Britain. He named it New South Wales. His naturalist, Joseph Banks, collected so many previously unknown plants that Cook decided to call his landing place Botany Bay.

I'm an Austr-alien

Terra Australis

The first explorers of Australia were the Aborigines, whose ancestors made the earliest known sea voyages there from Asia more than 50,000 years ago. They learned how to live in a hot, dry landscape, finding water and food in unlikely places. European explorers began arriving from the 17th century, followed in the next century by settlers. They often looked down on Aborigines, who had few clothes or possessions, but the Aborigines were much better at surviving in the Australian "outback" (interior).

Tasman

The north coast of Australia was mapped in 1644 by Abel Tasman, a Dutch explorer. He was not impressed by Australia—then called New Holland—finding "nothing profitable, only poor naked people". On an earlier voyage in 1642–43, Tasman discovered New Zealand and Tasmania, which was later named after him.

Dreamtime painting

Aborigines believe that they share their land with spirit beings, who live in a parallel world they call the "dreamtime." They paint pictures of the spirit beings on rocks, decorating them with colored dots and circles.

That's the spirits!

New Zealand

Tasmania

What a devil

Settlers

The British founded a prison settlement on the east coast in 1788. Prisoners were soon followed by free settlers, who brought sheep and cattle with them and who farmed along the coasts. Towns developed in the 19th century, including Sydney, Melbourne, and Adelaide. These became bases from which to explore the interior.

Inland sea?

The rivers of Southeast Australia flowed inland from the mountains. This led to the hope that they might lead to an inland sea or fertile lake region. In 1828–30, the English explorer Charles Sturt traced the course of these rivers. He was disappointed to find that they only led south again, to the coast.

Going north

The most successful explorer of Australia was Scotsman John McDouall Stuart. He realized that the only way to travel was light and fast. Three of his six expeditions set off from Adelaide in southern Australia, and one of these became the first south-to-north crossing of the continent in 1861–62. His route was later used to lay a telegraph line.

Disaster

In 1860, Robert O'Hara Burke led a big expedition, with 24 camels and 23 horses, from Melbourne to the north coast. Unlike Stuart, he knew nothing of the outback. On the return journey, Burke and two companions starved to death. A fourth man, John King, was saved by Aborigines, who nursed him until searchers arrived.

Surviving the south

In 1840–41, Englishman Edward Eyre explored the south coast to the west of Adelaide, with an Aborigine friend named Wylie. They hoped to find grazing land, but they only found waterless desert. They survived by collecting dew from bushes, until they were eventually rescued by a French whaling ship.

Trapped by a creek

Still hoping to find an inland sea, Charles Sturt set off with a large expedition in 1844. This included 15 men, 11 horses, 30 bullocks, 200 sheep, and a boat. Instead of a sea, he found a scorching desert. He was trapped for seven months beside a sinking creek, until the rains finally came.

ASIA

PACIFIC OCEAN

INDIAN OCEAN

— Tasman (1642–43)
— Tasman (1644)
— Flinders (1801–03)
— Sturt (1828–30)

— Eyre (1839–43)
— Sturt (1844–46)
— Burke (1860–61)
— Stuart (1860)
— Stuart (1861)
— Stuart (1862)

AUSTRALIA

Sydney

Botany Bay

Adelaide

Melbourne

TASMANIA

NEW ZEALAND

INTO AFRICA

Although Europeans had known about Africa for thousands of years, it was one of the last continents that they explored. The risks were great and the rewards seemed few. In the north, there was the challenging Sahara Desert, while in the south, there were dangerous animals, hostile tribes, and tropical diseases. Despite this, from the late 18th century, a few brave explorers set off for the "White Man's Grave," as Africa was known.

Timbuktu triumph

A Scotsman named Alexander Gordon Laing crossed the Sahara Desert in 1825. He narrowly survived an attack by Tuareg tribesmen, reaching Timbuktu in August 1826. However, as he was leaving, he was murdered.

Search for Timbuktu

One goal of exploration was to find a glorious West African city called Timbuktu, documented by medieval Muslim travelers. It was said to be so wealthy that its houses were roofed with gold.

Traveling in disguise

In 1824, the French Geographical Society offered a big cash prize to the first European to reach Timbuktu and return alive. René Caillié, who spoke Arabic, decided to go there disguised as an Egyptian Muslim.

Big disappointment

René Caillié arrived in Timbuktu in April of 1828. He was disappointed by the city, which he described as "a mass of ill-looking houses built of earth." Back home, he won the prize, but his health never recovered from the journey.

Rocky rapids

On a second Niger journey in 1805, Mungo Park hoped to avoid trouble by staying in a boat. However, in April 1806, his boat got stuck on a rock while traveling down some rapids. Attacked by tribesmen, Park jumped overboard and drowned.

Daylight robbery

Among other hardships, Mungo Park became sick and was imprisoned for four months by a Muslim ruler. Worst of all, Park was robbed in August of 1796, in the middle of the rainy season. Thieves took his horse, belongings, and clothes!

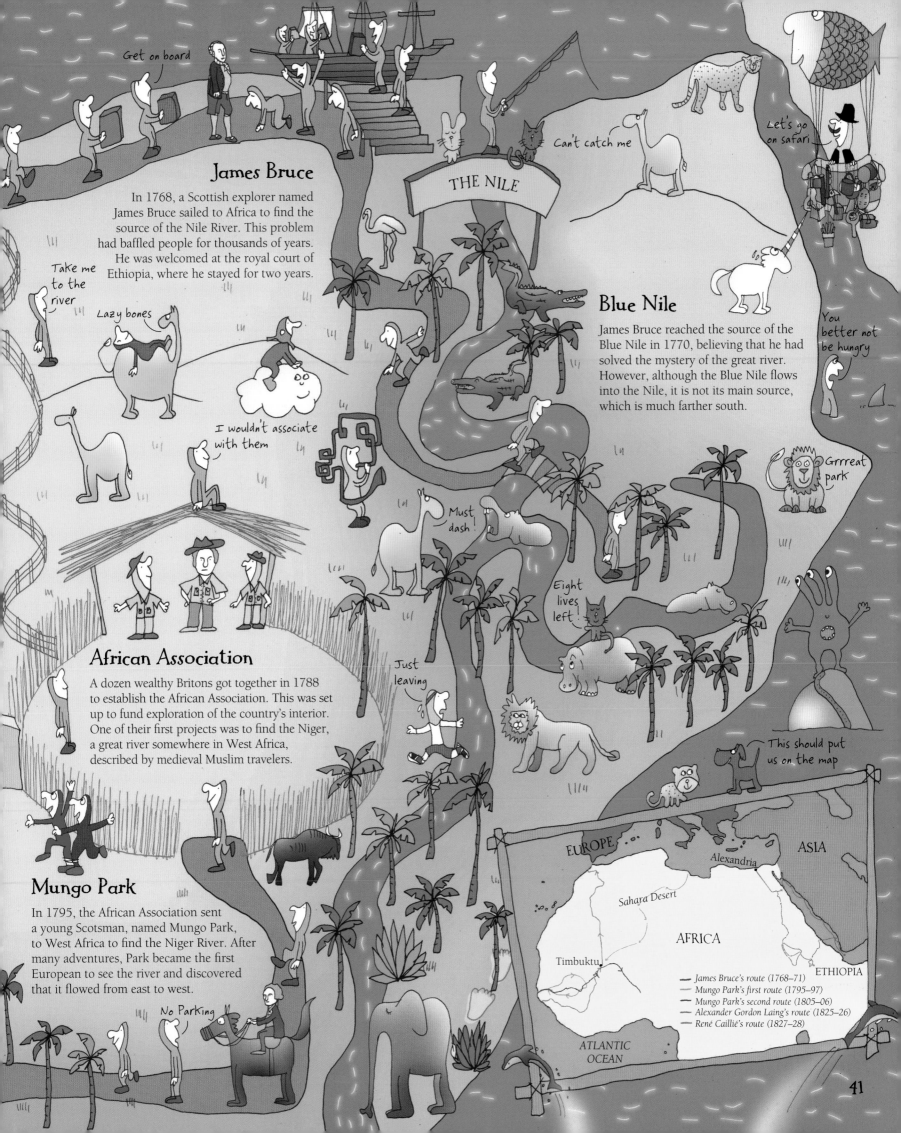

James Bruce

In 1768, a Scottish explorer named James Bruce sailed to Africa to find the source of the Nile River. This problem had baffled people for thousands of years. He was welcomed at the royal court of Ethiopia, where he stayed for two years.

Blue Nile

James Bruce reached the source of the Blue Nile in 1770, believing that he had solved the mystery of the great river. However, although the Blue Nile flows into the Nile, it is not its main source, which is much farther south.

African Association

A dozen wealthy Britons got together in 1788 to establish the African Association. This was set up to fund exploration of the country's interior. One of their first projects was to find the Niger, a great river somewhere in West Africa, described by medieval Muslim travelers.

Mungo Park

In 1795, the African Association sent a young Scotsman, named Mungo Park, to West Africa to find the Niger River. After many adventures, Park became the first European to see the river and discovered that it flowed from east to west.

— James Bruce's route (1768–71)
— Mungo Park's first route (1795–97)
— Mungo Park's second route (1805–06)
— Alexander Gordon Laing's route (1825–26)
— René Caillié's route (1827–28)

EUROPE
ASIA
Alexandria
Sahara Desert
AFRICA
Timbuktu
ETHIOPIA
ATLANTIC OCEAN

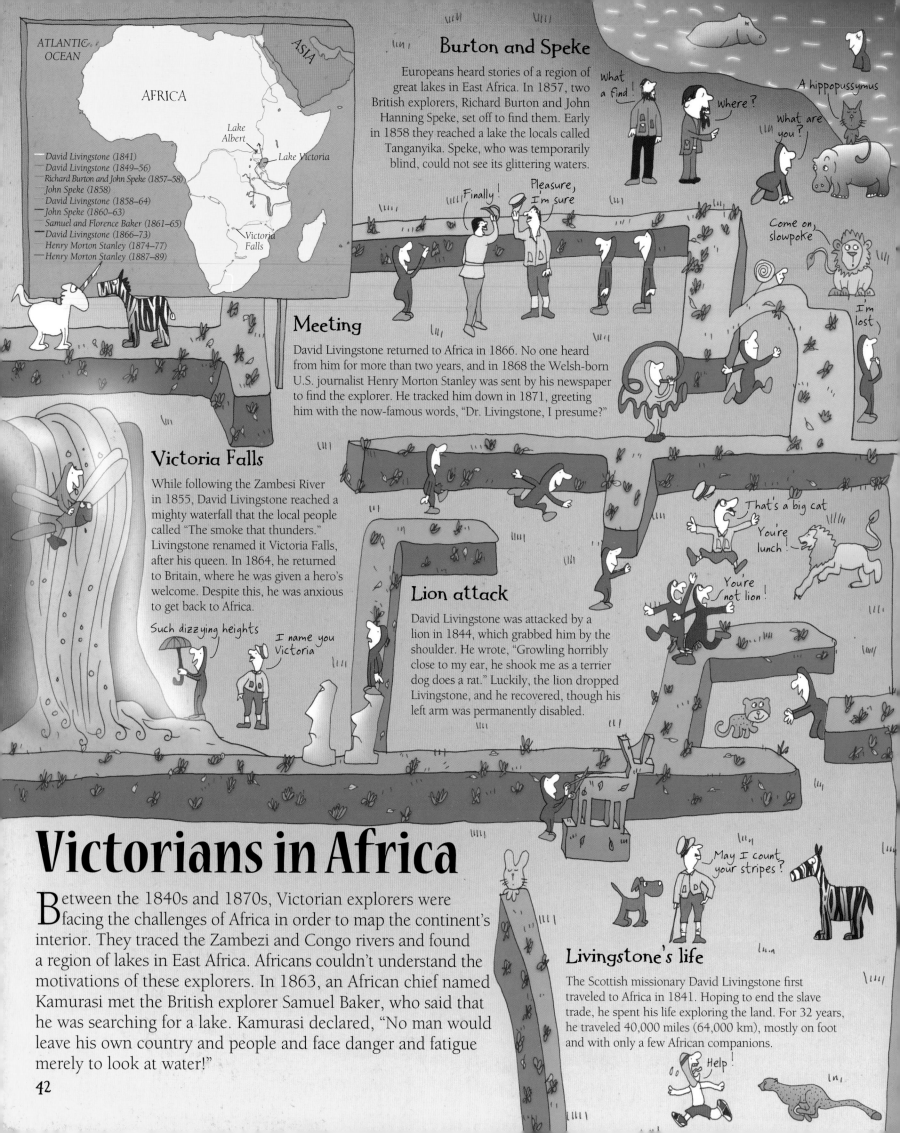

Burton and Speke

Europeans heard stories of a region of great lakes in East Africa. In 1857, two British explorers, Richard Burton and John Hanning Speke, set off to find them. Early in 1858 they reached a lake the locals called Tanganyika. Speke, who was temporarily blind, could not see its glittering waters.

Meeting

David Livingstone returned to Africa in 1866. No one heard from him for more than two years, and in 1868 the Welsh-born U.S. journalist Henry Morton Stanley was sent by his newspaper to find the explorer. He tracked him down in 1871, greeting him with the now-famous words, "Dr. Livingstone, I presume?"

Victoria Falls

While following the Zambesi River in 1855, David Livingstone reached a mighty waterfall that the local people called "The smoke that thunders." Livingstone renamed it Victoria Falls, after his queen. In 1864, he returned to Britain, where he was given a hero's welcome. Despite this, he was anxious to get back to Africa.

Lion attack

David Livingstone was attacked by a lion in 1844, which grabbed him by the shoulder. He wrote, "Growling horribly close to my ear, he shook me as a terrier dog does a rat." Luckily, the lion dropped Livingstone, and he recovered, though his left arm was permanently disabled.

Victorians in Africa

Between the 1840s and 1870s, Victorian explorers were facing the challenges of Africa in order to map the continent's interior. They traced the Zambezi and Congo rivers and found a region of lakes in East Africa. Africans couldn't understand the motivations of these explorers. In 1863, an African chief named Kamurasi met the British explorer Samuel Baker, who said that he was searching for a lake. Kamurasi declared, "No man would leave his own country and people and face danger and fatigue merely to look at water!"

Livingstone's life

The Scottish missionary David Livingstone first traveled to Africa in 1841. Hoping to end the slave trade, he spent his life exploring the land. For 32 years, he traveled 40,000 miles (64,000 km), mostly on foot and with only a few African companions.

The map legend:

- David Livingstone (1841)
- David Livingstone (1849–56)
- Richard Burton and John Speke (1857–58)
- John Speke (1858)
- David Livingstone (1858–64)
- John Speke (1860–63)
- Samuel and Florence Baker (1861–65)
- David Livingstone (1866–73)
- Henry Morton Stanley (1874–77)
- Henry Morton Stanley (1887–89)

Lake Victoria

Richard Burton then became sick and was unable to travel. On a solo mission, Speke headed north to another great lake, which he named Lake Victoria, after the British queen. He was sure that this was the source of the Nile River. Burton thought that Speke was wrong, and they became bitter enemies.

Source of the Nile

In 1860, Speke returned to explore Lake Victoria and found the Nile River flowing out of its north end. He went home, planning to confront Burton with this evidence in a public debate. On the day of the meeting, Speke shot himself, perhaps by accident, while hunting.

Married mission

During the 1860s, Samuel and Florence Baker, a husband and wife team, were also looking for the source of the Nile. In 1864, they found another great lake, north of Victoria, with waters also flowing into the Nile. They named this Lake Albert, after Queen Victoria's husband.

Congo expedition

After finding Livingstone, Henry Morton Stanley became an African explorer in his own right. From 1876, he traced the entire course of the Congo River. While Livingstone traveled light, Stanley had an army of 350 African porters, carrying supplies including a portable steamboat.

Congo battles

The African tribes who lived by the Congo River saw the arrival of Stanley's huge expedition as an invasion. As a result, Stanley had to fight 32 fierce battles along the river, losing more than half his men. By tracing the Congo River, Stanley had solved the last great mystery of African exploration.

43

Scientist explorers

The desire for scientific knowledge became a powerful new motive for exploration by the late 18th century. Scientist explorers traveled to remote lands, where they identified previously unknown plant and animal species. They brought back specimens for museums and gardens and made amazing discoveries about the workings of the natural world.

Humboldt

In 1799, the German scientist Alexander von Humboldt spent five years exploring 6,000 miles (9,600 km) of northwest South America. With his companion Aimé Bonpland, he collected plant and animal specimens and studied geology, ocean currents, weather patterns, and the magnetism of Earth.

SOUTH AMERICA

Recorded findings

On returning to Europe, Humboldt spent 20 years publishing the results of his expedition in 34 huge illustrated volumes. These writings inspired younger naturalists, including Charles Darwin, who described Humboldt as "the greatest scientific traveler who ever lived."

Darwin

In 1831, the British naturalist Charles Darwin set sail on a naval survey ship, *HMS Beagle*. For five years, Darwin traveled the coast of South America and explored the Galapagos Islands. He discovered that the island birds, though related to South American ones, were different species.

Finches

In the Galapagos Islands, Darwin discovered 13 species of finch, each with different shaped beaks, adapted for the food available on its island. Darwin concluded that they had all descended from the same species of South American finch, but they had evolved into different species.

Natural selection

Darwin realized that, within a species, individual animals vary slightly from each other. Those born with features better suited to their environment are more likely to survive to have offspring. Their features will be passed on to their young. As small changes build up, new species appear in a process he called "natural selection".

The Origin of Species

Although Darwin came up with his theory in 1838, he did not publish it until 1859, after learning that a fellow British naturalist, Alfred Russell Wallace, had come up with the same idea. Darwin's book, *The Origin of Species*, was an instant bestseller.

GALAPAGOS ISLANDS

Do I know you?

One of my feathered friends

Surely my bag will come out soon!

Slippery sucker

Is this terminal two?

Who is the bookworm?

A little light reading

Wish I could evolve some wheels

You'd look good in my living room

Let's sail that thing!

Sign here, please

Wonder where were going

It's rude to stare

44

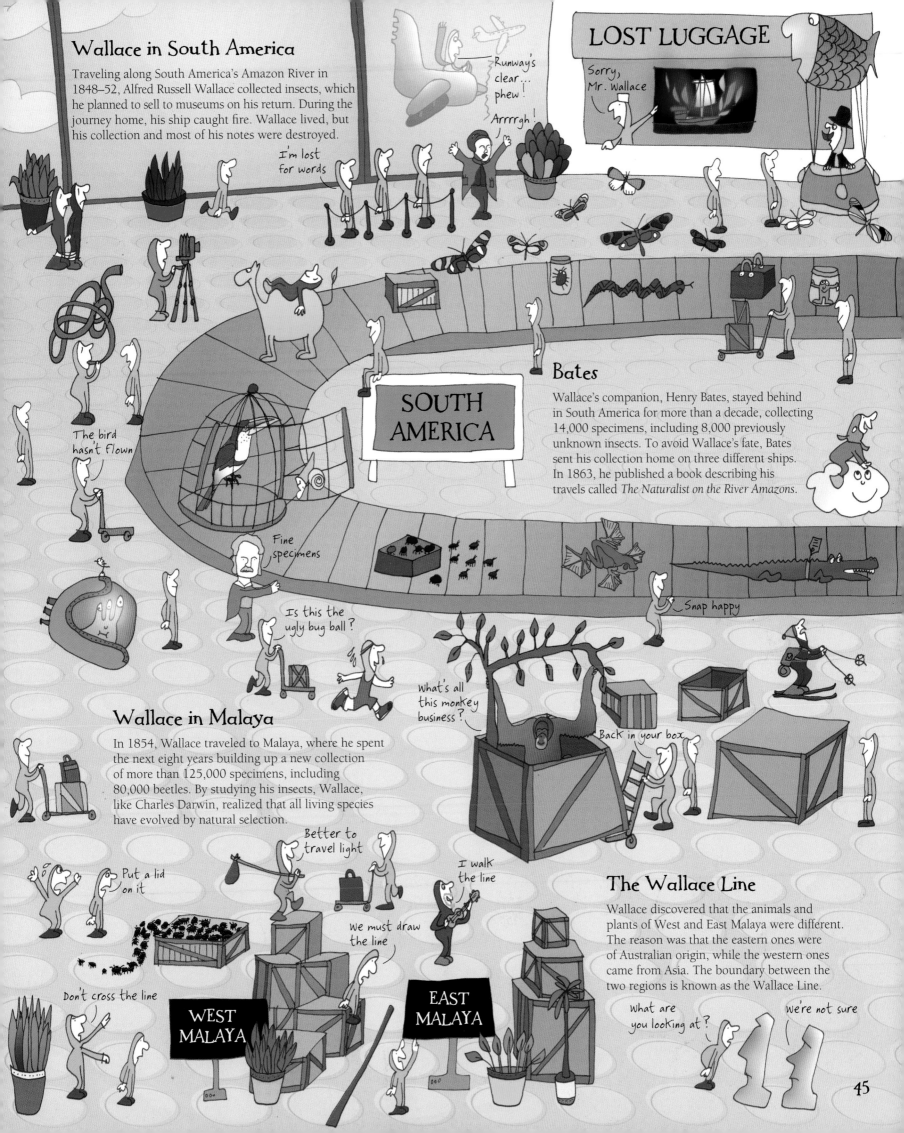

Wallace in South America

Traveling along South America's Amazon River in 1848–52, Alfred Russell Wallace collected insects, which he planned to sell to museums on his return. During the journey home, his ship caught fire. Wallace lived, but his collection and most of his notes were destroyed.

LOST LUGGAGE

Sorry, Mr. Wallace

Runway's clear... phew!

Arrrrgh!

I'm lost for words

SOUTH AMERICA

The bird hasn't flown

Fine specimens

Is this the ugly bug ball?

Bates

Wallace's companion, Henry Bates, stayed behind in South America for more than a decade, collecting 14,000 specimens, including 8,000 previously unknown insects. To avoid Wallace's fate, Bates sent his collection home on three different ships. In 1863, he published a book describing his travels called *The Naturalist on the River Amazons*.

Snap happy

What's all this monkey business?

Back in your box

Wallace in Malaya

In 1854, Wallace traveled to Malaya, where he spent the next eight years building up a new collection of more than 125,000 specimens, including 80,000 beetles. By studying his insects, Wallace, like Charles Darwin, realized that all living species have evolved by natural selection.

Better to travel light

Put a lid on it

We must draw the line

I walk the line

The Wallace Line

Wallace discovered that the animals and plants of West and East Malaya were different. The reason was that the eastern ones were of Australian origin, while the western ones came from Asia. The boundary between the two regions is known as the Wallace Line.

Don't cross the line

WEST MALAYA

EAST MALAYA

What are you looking at?

We're not sure

NORTH POLE

A major challenge for explorers in the 19th century was reaching the treacherous North Pole. This is the most northern point on the planet, located in the middle of a huge frozen ocean called the Arctic Ocean. Like other oceans, the Arctic has powerful currents, which make the ice sheets move, so it is very difficult to travel there.

Sledding backward

A British naval officer named William Parry tried to reach the North Pole by sled in 1827. Setting off from the Norwegian island of Spitzbergen, he gave up after discovering that the ice sheets were moving south faster than he could travel north.

Frozen in

Norwegian Fridtjof Nansen was a man with a plan in 1893. He allowed his strengthened ship, *Fram*, to be frozen into the ice, hoping that the Arctic currents would carry him to the North Pole. *Fram* spent three years in the ice but drifted south of Nansen's goal.

Lost toes

In the early 1900s, U.S. explorer Robert Peary tried eight times to get to the North Pole. On the first attempt, he lost eight toes to frostbite. Peary told his shocked traveling companion, Matthew Henson, "A few toes aren't much to achieve the Pole!"

Pole rivalry

In 1909, Robert Peary and a rival U.S. explorer, Frederick Cook, each claimed to have reached the North Pole. At the time, people believed Peary and not Cook. However, modern experts argue that Peary could not have reached the North Pole within the time he said.

Further conquests

Although no one knows for certain who got to the North Pole first, it has been visited several times since Robert Peary's day by airship, aircraft, and even by submarine. The first definite land crossing was made in 1968 by U.S. explorer Ralph Plaisted, who traveled in a snowmobile.

EUROPE

NORTH AMERICA

Spitzbergen

● North Pole

GREENLAND

ATLANTIC OCEAN

— William Parry (1827)
— Fridtjof Nansen (1893–96)
— Robert Peary (1909)

I win

Fibber!

I'm just a little husky

Do you have a sore throat?

My lips are sealed

You blockhead

I'm getting cold feet

Another Fram mess you got us into!

Can you seal this crack?

Cracking stuff

We're not in Pole position

What's in the deep freeze?

Fish sticks

Give me a lift

Plenty of bite, please

Are you impersonating me?

This is a breeze!

We're having a whale of a time

SOUTH POLE

To reach the South Pole, explorers had to cross icy Antarctica, the coldest and windiest place on Earth. Another problem was that the pole sits on a high plateau, around 9,800 ft (3,000 m) above sea level. Although it is the fifth-largest continent, Antarctica is so far from inhabited land that it was only discovered in the 18th century.

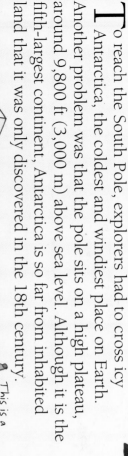

Ice ice baby

The southern continent

The existence of an Antarctic continent was discovered by Captain James Cook, who sailed around it from 1772. Although he did not see the continent itself, he knew that it must be there from the many icebergs, which only form on land.

This is a snow-go area

Ross Ice Shelf

In 1838, James Clark Ross led a British naval expedition, mapping most of the Antarctic coastline. Over five years, he discovered two volcanoes and an ice shelf the size of France connected to the continent. This was later named the Ross Ice Shelf in his honor.

Antarctica leaves me cold

Very icy, too

To the South Pole

The first attempt to reach the South Pole was by the British explorer Robert Falcon Scott, in 1902–03. He gave up when a companion, Ernest Shackleton, became sick with scurvy. Leading a second expedition in 1908, Shackleton got within 480 miles (770 km) of the pole.

So near ... and yet so far

This place gives me the chills

Freeze frame

Race to the pole

By 1910, the quest for the South Pole had become a race between a Norwegian expedition, led by Roald Amundsen, and another British expedition, headed by Robert Falcon Scott. Using excellent skiers and dog sleds, Amundsen won, reaching the Pole on December 12, 1911.

I've been left out in the cold

Down and out

Scott's team dragged their sled to the pole themselves, making the journey much harder. They arrived on January 17, 1912 to find the Norwegian flag already flying. They died on the return journey, weakened by frostbite, scurvy, and exhaustion.

I'm dog tired

Pipped at the Pole

oh, snow!

SOUTH AMERICA

PACIFIC OCEAN

ROSS SEA

ANTARCTICA

• South Pole

Ross Ice Shelf

NEW ZEALAND

AUSTRALIA

INDIAN OCEAN

— James Clark Ross (1838–41)
— James Clark Ross (1841–43)
— Roald Amundsen (1910–11)
— Robert Falcon Scott (1910–12)

47

Ocean depths

Although deep oceans cover most of Earth's surface, little was known about them until the 19th century. People believed that the deep sea was too cold and the water pressure too great for anything to live there. With the 1872 voyage of the British research ship *HMS Challenger*, the new science of oceanography was born. During a four-year voyage of exploration, *HMS Challenger* found mountains, trenches, and a seabed teeming with life.

HMS Challenger

This British naval warship was converted into a floating laboratory. Equipped with bottles for seawater samples, weighted ropes for measuring depths, and dredging nets for scooping up sea life, *HMS Challenger*'s mission was "to find out everything about the sea."

Back off, fish face

New species

HMS Challenger was a success story, finding 4,717 previously unknown species of marine life. New discoveries included fish with huge eyes and fish able to create their own light, both adaptations to help them live in the dark depths.

You look out of plaice

All going swimmingly

Sound mapping

From the late 1940s, the seabeds were mapped using sonar. This technology works by sending sound waves down from a surface ship and recording the echo that is sent back. Using sonar, oceanographers mapped the world's ridges and trenches and discovered that they matched areas where earthquakes and volcanoes were common.

Super sound effects

I won't take the bait

Hook, line, and sinker

Name that tuna?

Bathysphere

The U.S. inventor and diver Frederick Otis Barton created a craft for exploring the sea in 1928. Called the bathysphere, it was lowered from a ship on a cable and carried a crew of two. The bathysphere made its first descent into the ocean in 1930.

Some bunny help me

Just in time for the seafood special

Hydrothermal vents

In the 1970s, the U.S. manned submersible, *Alvin*, explored hydrothermal vents—hot springs on the seabed where mineral-rich fluids flow from Earth's crust. Even there, many new creatures were found, including strange fish, crabs, and shrimp.

Tubeworms

One of the most bizarre creatures found living by the hydrothermal vents was the tubeworm, which grows up to 8 ft (2.4 m) in length.

Tubeworm

Undersea mountains

In the middle of the Atlantic Ocean, *HMS Challenger* discovered a large ridge running from the Arctic to the South Atlantic. Called the Mid-Atlantic Ridge, this is the longest mountain chain on Earth.

Bathyscaphe

Following on from the bathysphere was the bathyscaphe of the 1940s. A Swiss scientist named Auguste Piccard invented this new deep-sea diving submarine. Unlike the bathysphere, the bathyscaphe did not need to be tethered to a surface vessel, so there was huge opportunity for underwater exploration.

Seismic exploration

Today, geologists probe the seabed using seismic exploration. This involves setting off explosions or transmitting vibrations from ships. Shock waves travel underground and are then reflected back by different materials beneath the seabed. The method, invented in the 1930s for use on land, is now used to find undersea oil and gas deposits.

Surface ship

Signal is transmitted from the ship

Sound detectors, towed behind the ship, pick up the echoes

SEISMIC EXPLORATION

Changing Earth

Studies of the seabed reveal that Earth's surface is made up of around a dozen great plates, positioned on top of molten rock. Ridges form when plates move apart and molten rock flows up, forming new land, while, at the trenches, one plate is pushed beneath another.

Trieste

In 1960, Auguste Piccard's son, Jacques, took the bathyscaphe *Trieste* down 35,814 ft (10,916 m) to the bottom of the Pacific Ocean's Marianas Trench, the deepest point in the ocean. It took Piccard and crewmember Don Walsh more than three hours to return to the surface.

Arggh! Monster of the deep

I've got bigger fish to fry

I've earned my water wings

Is that a flying fish?

We're going to school!

Cod on, then

Cracks are starting to show

That's deep, man

Given to me on a plate

I'm at my lowest point

MOUNTAIN PEAKS

In the 18th century, Europeans began to embrace the challenge of climbing mountains. Initially, these climbers were scientists, who wanted to carry out research. Later, people were driven by the desire to be the first to climb particular peaks. Mountaineers started by climbing the Alps of Europe. Once these mountains had all been conquered, they turned to the Himalayas of Asia—a range that includes Mount Everest, the world's highest mountain. When English mountaineer George Mallory was asked why he wanted to climb Mount Everest, he replied, "Because it's there!"

I have a sweet tooth

Just add a light dusting of snow

Blanc blindness

The highest mountain in the Alps is Mont Blanc, which rises up 15,780 ft (4,810 m) above sea level. It was first climbed in 1786 by a French doctor named Michel-Gabriel Paccard, with his guide, Jacques Balmat. Dazzled by the bright snow, both men went temporarily blind during the climb.

Measuring the mountain

Paccard climbed Mont Blanc for scientific reasons. He wanted to figure out the mountain's height using a barometer—an instrument for measuring air pressure. Paccard hoped to prove that it was the tallest mountain in Europe. Unfortunately, when he got to the top, he found that his barometer was broken!

Sugar storm ahead!

This is the cherry on the cake

Watch out!

I need a brrr-ometer

I can't see, and it's snow joke

Climbing for fun

During the 1850s, British tourists on vacation in the Alps began climbing them for fun. The fashion started in 1854, when a young English lawyer named Alfred Wills climbed the 12,112-ft- (3,692-m)- high Wetterhorn. Wills celebrated by planting a fir tree at the top. Over the next ten years, 50 more alpine peaks were conquered.

It's in peak condition

Avalanche!

I'm in choc!

I can't do heights

Basic equipment

Victorian climbers only had basic mountaineering equipment. This included ropes to tie themselves together, ice axes to cut steps in the snow, and long walking sticks with metal spikes, called alpenstocks. They dressed in the same heavy tweed clothes that they would wear for a walk in the countryside.

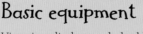

All set, boys?

On top of the world

In 1953, New Zealander Edmund Hillary and Sherpa Tenzing Norgay participated in an English expedition to conquer Mount Everest. On May 29, the two climbers reached the summit, where they hugged each other with joy. Tenzing buried candy at the top, as an offering to the mountain.

Matterhorn mishap

The deadliest mountain in the Alps is the Matterhorn. It was first climbed in 1865 by the English mountaineer Edward Whymper, with six other men. Coming back down, one climber slipped and fell off the slope, pulling three others to their deaths. Whymper and two guides only survived because the rope attaching them to the others snapped.

Sherpa guides

Mountaineers in the Himalayas hired the local people, called Sherpas, to be their guides and porters. With lungs suited to the thin air, Sherpas are excellent climbers. They see Mount Everest as a holy place and call it *Chomolungma* ("Goddess Mother of the World").

Frozen in time

In the 1920s, English climber George Mallory took part in three Everest expeditions. During the last, in 1924, he disappeared close to the summit, along with his companion, Andrew Irvine. It was not until 1999 that Mallory's frozen body was found on the mountain. No one knows whether he reached the top before he died.

Himalayan heights

The tallest mountains on Earth are the Himalayas, situated between India and China. Highest of all is Mount Everest, reaching 29,028 ft (8,848 m) above sea level. Climbing is made difficult by the strong winds, freezing cold, and reduced oxygen in the air. From 1924, climbers used bottled oxygen to help them breathe at this high altitude.

Fallen heroes

Many mountaineers did not reach the Matterhorn's summit of 14,780 ft (4,504 m). The difficulty of climbing the sheer faces and battling frequent falls of rock and snow caused many casualties. Since 1865, more than 500 climbers have been killed trying to climb the mountain.

Space probes

Unmanned craft, commonly called space probes, are sent into space to take photographs of parts of our solar system. Probes have now been launched by the U.S.A., Russia, China, the European Union, Japan, and India. They have photographed the other planets, their moons, comets, and asteroids.

JUNE 2004

SpaceShipOne

The first privately funded spacecraft was SpaceShipOne, a rocket-powered plane funded by U.S. multimillionaire Paul Allen. In 2004, U.S. pilot Mike Melvill became the first commercial astronaut on SpaceShipOne. Several companies are now developing spacecraft to fly private citizens to space.

SpaceShipOne offers passengers six minutes of weightlessness on an edge-of-space trip

The ISS consists of 18 major parts, which were launched separately and assembled in space

I'm over the Moon!

We've won!

International Space Station

The 1990s saw the start of a new era of international cooperation in space exploration. The U.S.A., Russia, Japan, Canada, and the European Union joined together to build the International Space Station, which began construction in 1998. This space laboratory orbits Earth and is continually manned by astronauts.

NOV. 1998

One small step

While Collins stayed on board the command module, Armstrong and Aldrin took the landing module down to the Moon, where they landed safely on July 20, 1969. As he stepped onto the lunar surface, Armstrong famously said, "That's one small step for (a) man, one giant leap for mankind." The U.S. had won the space race by landing men on the Moon.

When the Moon hits your eye like a big pizza pie, that's... painful

JULY 1969

Moon mission

On July 16, 1969, around 600 million people around the world watched the live television broadcast of the launch of Apollo 11, the U.S. Moon mission. The spacecraft carried three astronauts, Neil Armstrong, Edwin "Buzz" Aldrin, and Michael Collins. After three days in space, the astronauts reached the Moon.

Apollo 11's rocket guzzled 3,500 gallons (13,000 litres) of fuel every second

Chinese in space

By the 1990s, China had joined the space race, launching a series of spacecraft. The first manned mission was Shenzhou 5, in 2003. Astronaut Yang Liwei made a 21-hour flight, completing 14 orbits of Earth. On his return, he was awarded the title of "Space Hero."

Shenzhou's reentry capsule could seat three crewmembers

OCT. 2003

Hubble telescope

In 1990, the U.S. launched a space telescope called Hubble. Orbiting outside Earth's atmosphere, which distorts and blocks light, Hubble has a much clearer view of space than telescopes on Earth have. It has sent back hundreds of thousands of pictures of distant parts of the universe.

Hubble is about the same size as a school bus

So-viet near yet so-viet far!

APR. 1990

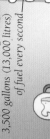
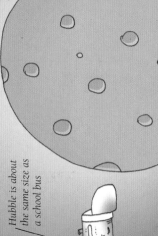
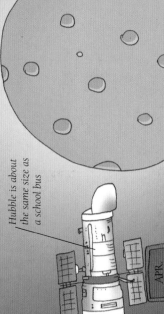

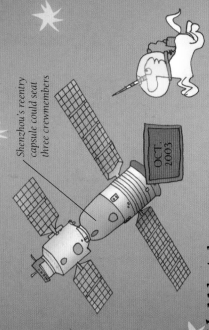
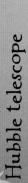

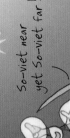

INTO SPACE

The world's two most powerful nations at the time, the U.S.A. and the Soviet Union (U.S.S.R.), began a race to explore space in the 1950s. Each superpower saw winning the race as a matter of national pride but also feared that the other might launch deadly weapons from space. It became the most expensive program of exploration in history, and its greatest achievement came in 1969, when the U.S.A. landed the first men on the Moon. Several other countries, and even private companies, have since begun to explore space.

NASA

The U.S.A. started their own space program in 1958, run by the National Aeronautics and Space Administration (NASA). Its chief designer was a German man named Wernher von Braun. Like Korolev, he had developed rockets as weapons during World War II.

U.S. space programs

From 1962, NASA organized three big space programs. The Mercury program put the first American, John Glenn, into orbit that same year. By 1964, the Gemini program was developing new methods for space travel, sending astronauts on longer flights. The Apollo program, from 1966–75, carried men to the Moon.

Titan rockets launched all of the Gemini missions

I need some space

You've lost a lot of weight lately

What a hit!

Stars and stripes!

It's hammer time!

Hurry up, they're going to win.

Take that!

Humans in space

In the early days, the U.S.S.R. seemed to be winning the space race. In 1961, Russian Yuri Gagarin became the first man to travel in space, on Vostok 1. In 1963, Valentina Tereshkova became the first woman in space on Vostok 6.

Mercury spacecraft were only big enough to fly one crewmember

Ham

In 1961, the U.S.A. sent a chimp named Ham into space. Ham successfully returned to Earth, with only a bruised nose.

Laika

Just one month after Sputnik 1, the U.S.S.R. launched Sputnik 2, which was the first spacecraft to carry a live passenger into orbit. This passenger was a dog named Laika, who sadly died soon after takeoff.

Sputnik 1

The Soviets raced out of the starting blocks in 1957, by launching the first man-made object into space. This was a satellite 23 in (58 cm) in diameter, called Sputnik 1. It orbited Earth, sending back radio signals for 22 days, before its batteries ran out.

Sputnik 1 burned up on reentry into Earth's atmosphere in 1958

Far out!

U.S.S.R.

The Soviet space program was headed by the excellent scientist Sergei Korolev, who had designed rocket weapons during World War II. His work was so secretive that his identity was not revealed until 1990, 24 years after his death. During his lifetime, he was known only as the "Chief Designer."

53

The future

We will continue to explore outer space in the future, sending missions to the planets and moons of our solar system, and perhaps even beyond. There is also a lot left to be discovered on Earth, where new living species continue to be identified.

2005
After a seven-year journey, the European Space Agency's Huygens probe lands on Titan, a moon of Saturn. This is the first landing on a moon other than Earth's.

1998
The Russians launch the first part of the International Space Station, a space laboratory orbiting Earth. It is used for scientific experiments by astronauts from many nations.

1961
Soviet cosmonaut Yuri Gagarin is the first man in space. Eight years later, U.S. astronauts Neil Armstrong and Edwin "Buzz" Aldrin become the first men on the Moon.

1960
Jacques Piccard and Don Walsh reach the deepest point on the seabed in the deep-sea diving vessel *Trieste*.

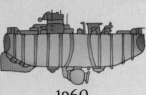

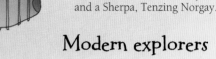

1953
A large British expedition climbs Mount Everest, the world's tallest mountain. The peak is reached by a New Zealander, Edmund Hillary, and a Sherpa, Tenzing Norgay.

Modern explorers

By the middle of the 20th century, the entire world had been mapped, yet explorers found new tests. The world's highest mountain was scaled, the deepest point in the seabed was reached, and there was a race to explore space.

1519
Ferdinand Magellan leads a Spanish fleet in the first crossing of the Pacific. He dies in the Philippines, but one ship completes the first voyage around the world.

Northern voyages

From the 16th century, the British and Dutch grew envious of the wealth of Spain and Portugal. They also tried to reach Asia, but instead by sailing northwest and northeast. However, explorers only found icy regions, and many died on their search for the northern passages.

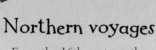

I should have brought a coat

1553
Sir Hugh Willoughby leads an English expedition in search of a northeast passage to Asia, but he freezes to death off Lapland.

1596
The Dutch seafarer Willem Barents sails in search of a northeast passage. He discovers and names Spitzbergen ("Jagged peaks") and spends winter on the Arctic islands of Novaya Zemlya, but he dies on his return journey.

Can't we be friends?

1610
English explorer Henry Hudson searches for a northwest passage. He sails into Hudson Bay, where his ship is trapped in ice. When the ice melts, his crew mutinies and abandons him.

Spice up my life

1498
Vasco da Gama, a Portuguese explorer, makes the first voyage from Europe to India, returning with a valuable cargo of spices. More than half his men die from scurvy.

Hi, guys

1492
Christopher Columbus, an Italian serving Spain, sails across the Atlantic Ocean and reaches the Caribbean Islands in 1492. He founds Hispaniola, the first European settlement in the Americas, a year later.

1487
The Portuguese seafarer, Bartolomeu Dias, sails around the southern tip of Africa, making the first European voyage into the Indian Ocean. This opens a sea route to India.

I'll put my neck on the line

1405
China sends out the first of six expeditions commanded by Zheng He, who visits lands in the Indian Ocean. His fleets include the largest wooden ships ever built, and he returns with exotic wonders, including a giraffe.

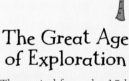

The Great Age of Exploration

The period from the 15th to early 16th centuries was the greatest era in world exploration. It began with Chinese voyages to the southern seas. Later, Portuguese and Spanish expeditions sailed to India, discovered America, and sailed all the way around the world.

Trip through time

Throughout the ages, there have been various motives for exploration. The Viking age saw sailors searching for new lands to settle. In the 15th century, Europeans sought a sea route to the wealth of Asia. Unraveling the mysteries of the universe is the main reason for exploration in modern times. One successful expedition or breakthrough can inspire other explorers to set off, ensuring more new ground is broken in the future.

Prehistoric age

Our ancestors were hunter-gatherers, who left Africa 70,000 years ago and set off in search of new lands to settle. At first, they stayed close to the warm tropics, moving east across Asia. Later, they found their way to Australia, Europe, and the Americas.

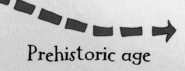

Water way to go!

c. 50,000 BCE
Australia is settled by people from Southeast Asia, who make the earliest known sea journey. They have to cross 56 miles (90 km) of open water to reach it.

Hello

I don't believe we've met

Polar exploration

From the late 19th century, exploration became a question of facing great challenges. The greatest of all were reaching the North and South poles, which are the most hostile places on Earth. Explorers raced to be the first to the poles and plant their country's flag there.

What's that, Skippy?

I lake it a lot

1872
HMS Challenger, a converted British Navy warship, sails around the world investigating the oceans. The expedition discovers undersea mountain ranges and finds life in the deep ocean.

1862
Scottish explorer John McDouall Stuart completes the first south-to-north crossing of Australia. His route is later used for a telegraph line and a road, the Stuart Highway.

1857
In West Africa, English explorers John Hanning Speke and Richard Burton reach the region of the Great Lakes. Speke discovers that one lake is the source of the Nile River and names it Lake Victoria after his queen.

1911
A Norwegian expedition, led by Roald Amundsen, and a British one, led by Robert Falcon Scott, both race to the South Pole. Amundsen, using dog sleds, is the winner.

1909
After eight attempts, U.S. explorer Robert Peary claims to have reached the North Pole. Given the short time that he took, it is unlikely that his claim was true.

-I'm very mappy

Ahhhh

I'm not your dentist

Victorian explorers

During the Victorian age, explorers traced rivers in Africa and crossed the Australian interior. There was a new attempt to find a northwest passage. Though it was unsuccessful, the expeditions led to the mapping of the Canadian Arctic.

The Scientific Age

In the late 18th century, expeditions were driven by a new thirst for scientific knowledge. Explorers of the time traveled with scientific observers, such as botanists. New scientific research societies sent out expeditions to fill in the spaces on the maps.

1768
Captain James Cook, a British explorer, sets sail on the first of three great voyages of exploration in the Pacific Ocean. He charts the east coast of Australia and discovers the Hawaiian Islands.

1796
A Scottish explorer named Mungo Park is the first European to see Africa's Niger River. He is sent by the African Association, a scientific body founded by wealthy Britons.

1799
The German scientist Alexander von Humboldt explores northwest South America, collecting data on geology, weather, butterflies, and plants. He inspires later scientific travelers, including Charles Darwin.

Have you seen my pants?

Take a Leif out of my book

The Middle Ages

The greatest explorers of the early Middle Ages were the Vikings of Scandinavia, who sailed west across the North Sea and Atlantic Ocean, discovering and settling new lands. In the later Middle Ages, Europeans traveled east along the Silk Road, a trade route linking China to the Mediterranean world.

1324
Ibn Battuta, a Muslim scholar from Morocco, sets out on the first of many journeys in Asia, as well as East and West Africa. He travels at least 75,000 miles (120,000 km) during 30 years of traveling.

1271
The explorer Marco Polo of Italy travels east to China along the Silk Road. After 24 years of exploration, he describes the lands that he has visited in a famous book.

c. 980 CE
Erik the Red, a Norwegian settler in Iceland, explores and settles Greenland. About 20 years later, his son Leif Erikson reaches a region of North America that he calls Vinland.

c. 865 CE
A Norwegian Viking named Floki Raven explores and names Iceland, after spending a cold winter there. Soon, settlers arrive from Norway.

Which way now?

Trade like the winds!

Brrr!

Ancient explorers

The earliest explorers that we know by name were the ancient Egyptians, Greeks, and Phoenicians. These were trading peoples, searching for goods such as metals and spices. After exploring the Mediterranean Sea, they sailed north into the Atlantic Ocean, and south around Africa.

c. 16,000 BCE
America is settled by hunters from Asia. They follow herds of animals over a land bridge between the two continents.

c. 1470 BCE
Queen Hatshepsut of Egypt sends a fleet of ships on a trading mission to Punt, somewhere in East Africa. This is the first recorded expedition.

c. 600 BCE
Phoenician explorers sail clockwise all the way around Africa for Pharaoh Necho II of Egypt. It takes almost three years to complete their journey.

c. 310 BCE
The Greek explorer Pytheas sails around Britain and reaches a northern land that he calls Thule. This is probably Iceland or Norway. He writes that the midsummer Sun does not set there.

Unknown future

A century ago, no one thought that people could travel to the Moon. In the same way, we cannot know exactly where explorers will travel in the future. Perhaps one day, it may even be possible to travel through time or to distant galaxies.

On to Mars

Another NASA plan is to send a rocket to Mars and back, bringing samples collected by robotic vehicles. Mars once had water and may have even had life. The aim is to learn if there was life on Mars in the past and what happened to it.

Back to the Moon

As part of its new Constellation mission, NASA is building a fleet of rockets to return astronauts to the Moon—and hopefully to allow them to spend long periods of time living there. Learning to live on the Moon is preparation for further space exploration.

Tracking comets

The extinction of the dinosaurs, around 65 million years ago, was probably caused by a comet or asteroid hitting Earth. One practical reason for future space exploration is to track comets and asteroids and to deflect them if they are on course for our planet.

Life in space

One goal of space exploration is to see if there is life on other planets and moons. The most likely place to find life is on Europa, a moon of Jupiter, which is thought to have an ice-covered ocean. A joint European/NASA mission to Europa is planned for 2020.

I need to get a life

Eureka!

I think you meant Europa

Tree navigation

Rainforests are home to millions of unknown species of animals, plants, and insects. The hardest area to study is the canopy (top level) of the trees. Using a new technology called dendronautics (tree navigation), scientists can now study the canopy, by traveling in small airships.

At the top of my game

Antarctic lake

One of the world's largest lakes was recently discovered beneath the ice sheets covering Antarctica. The water of Lake Vostok is one million years old. Russian scientists plan to send a robot probe, called a cryobot, into the lake in order to see if life exists there.

Heating its way through the ice, the cryobot takes measurements and collects data

Deep breath!

Dive in!

Can I borrow someone's flippers?

Ocean creatures

Most of the world's marine life remains a mystery. New species of large sea creatures, including beaked whales, are still being discovered. Future explorers may find that creatures that were thought to be legendary, such as the giant sea serpent, really exist.

I'm the stuff of legends

Are you for real?

Keep up.

Super squids

The giant squid and colossal squid are two huge species that live in the deep ocean, where they are hunted by sperm whales. So far, only dead specimens have been found of these squids. It is hoped that one day these remarkable creatures will be captured on film.

It's all come to a head

Not that giant compared to me!

FUTURE EXPLORATION

Today, we can see satellite photographs of almost anywhere on Earth via the Internet. It may seem like there is nowhere left to explore, but in reality, there is a lot left to discover—in the oceans, in the rainforests, and under Antarctica's ice sheets. This is also the start of a new era of space exploration, with plans to return to the Moon and to travel to other planets.

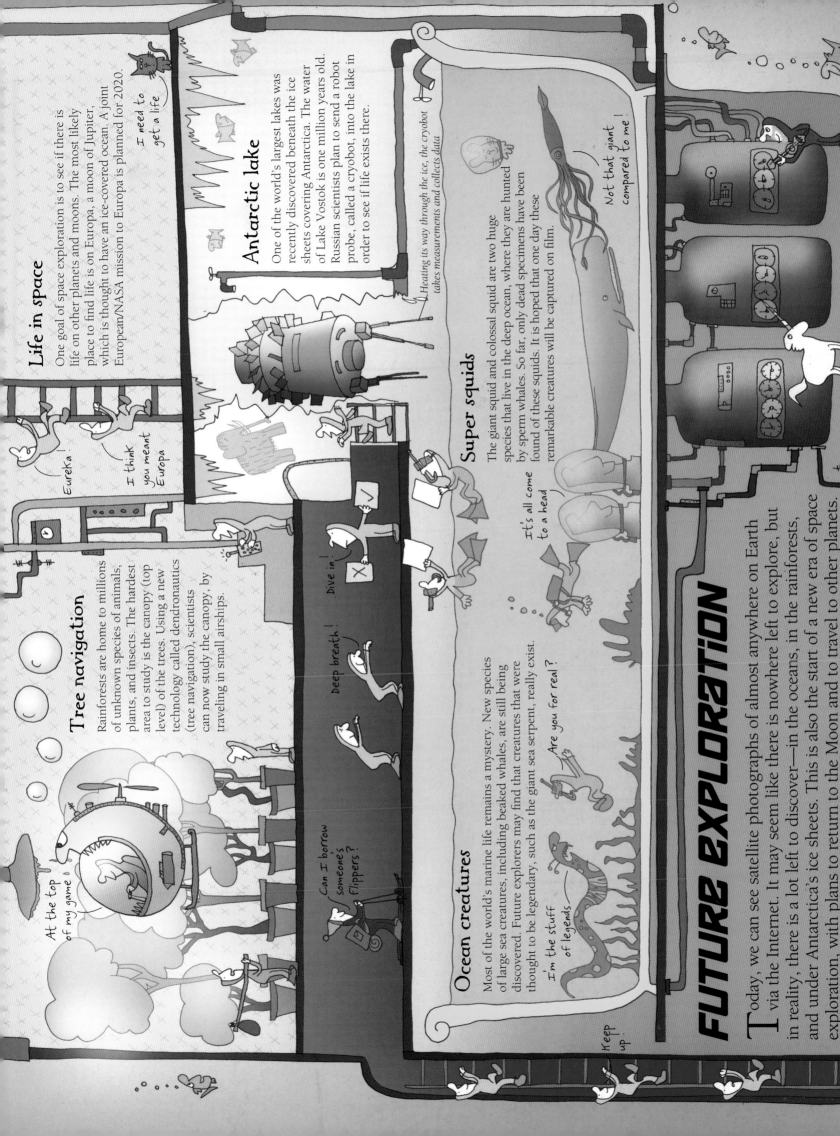

GLOSSARY

Aborigines
The name given by British settlers to the native people of Australia. It means "original inhabitants" in Latin.

African Association
A club set up in 1788 by a group of wealthy Britons to organize the exploration of Africa.

Amber
The fossilized resin of ancient trees. It has been highly prized since ancient times for use in jewelery.

Antarctic
The cold, southernmost region of Earth, surrounding the South Pole.

Apollo program
A U.S. space program that ran from 1966 to 1975 and sent 12 astronauts to the Moon.

Arctic
The cold, northernmost region of Earth, surrounding the North Pole.

Asteroid
An object orbiting the Sun, usually between Mars and Jupiter, in a region called the asteroid belt. Asteroids are made of rock or metal.

Astrolabe
An instrument for measuring latitude from the height of the Sun at noon.

Astronaut
The U.S. term for a crewmember of a spacecraft. It derives from two Greek words, *astron* (star) and *nautes* (sailor).

Aztecs
A warlike Mexican people, whose empire lasted from the early 14th century until 1521, when they were conquered by the Spanish.

Barometer
An instrument for measuring air pressure—the weight of the invisible gases in Earth's atmosphere. Early barometers used a column of mercury in a tube, which rose or fell according to the air pressure.

Bathyscaphe
A craft for deep-sea diving, invented in the 1940s by August Piccard. Unlike a bathysphere, it is self-propelled and not connected to a surface vessel. Its name in Greek means "ship of the deep."

Bathysphere
A spherical craft for deep-sea diving. It is not powered but is lowered into the sea from a surface vessel.

Blue Nile
The Blue Nile is the shorter of two rivers that join together to form the Nile, the longest river on Earth. It flows from Lake Tana in Ethiopia to Khartoum in the Sudan, where it joins the White Nile.

Botanist
A scientist who specializes in the study of plants.

Cape
A point or head of land that sticks out into the sea.

Caravan
A group of travelers journeying together for safety.

Caravel
A Portuguese ship with lateen (triangular) sails, used for voyages of exploration in the 15th century.

Carrack
A large European trading ship with square sails. Carracks were used from the 15th to the 16th centuries.

Comet
An object made from ice, dust, and rocky particles orbiting the Sun.

Conquistador
The Spanish word for a conqueror, specifically referring to the 16th-century Spanish conquerors of the native peoples of Central and South America.

Cosmonaut
The Russian term for a crewmember of a spacecraft. It derives from two Greek words, *kosmos* (universe) and *nautes* (sailor).

Cryobot
A robot-controlled probe, designed to penetrate ice sheets. It has a heated tip for melting the ice.

Dead reckoning
A way of figuring out a ship's position by recording its speed and direction and marking the course traveled on a chart.

Dreamtime
The Australian aboriginal name for the time of the creation of the world by spirit beings.

Empire
A large area, including different peoples, ruled by a single state. There have been many empires throughout history, usually created by military conquest.

European Space Agency
A European organization established in 1975 to carry out space exploration. It currently has 18 member nations.

Evolution
The process of gradual development of species over time.

Exploration
The search for unknown lands or places or new routes to known lands.

Friar
A member of a Roman Catholic religious brotherhood. A friar's main role was to preach, but they also served as teachers and ambassadors for medieval European rulers.

Frostbite
This condition occurs when human body tissues freeze in cold temperatures. The most vulnerable areas are the ears, nose, cheeks, fingers, and toes. It can lead to amputation of the affected part.

Gemini program
A U.S. space program that ran from 1964 to 1966, which prepared the way for Moon missions.

Geography
The study of Earth's surface. The name in Greek means "writing about Earth."

Geology
The study of Earth's crust. Geologists study how rocks, oil, and gas form.

Hubble Space Telescope
A space telescope launched in 1990, which orbits Earth. It is named after the U.S. astronomer Edwin Hubble. Outside Earth's atmosphere, the telescope can see farther and more clearly than telescopes on the ground.

Hydrothermal vent
A crack in the seabed, where hot gases flow up from Earth's crust, heating the surrounding water.

Incas
The native people of Peru, who ruled a great empire from the 1430s until the 16th century, when they were conquered by the Spanish.

Incense
A substance from the gum and resin of certain trees, which produces sweet-smelling smoke when burned.

International Space Station
A space laboratory that orbits Earth. Its first part was launched by the Russians in 1998. It is a joint project between the U.S.A., Russia, Japan, Canada, and the European Union.

Inuit
The native people of the Canadian Arctic and Greenland. The name comes from the Inuit language and simply means "human beings."

Junk
A Chinese ocean-going ship with a flat bottom and sails that are often square and stiffened with bamboo.

Khan
The title of a ruler in Mongolian and in other central Asian languages.

Lateen
A triangular sail.

Latitude
A position to the north or south of the equator, which is an imaginary line around the middle of Earth.

I'm lost for words   I've broken down   I can't see the point   That's enough of your latitude   Words are all I have...

Longitude
A position to the east or west of a given point. Today, we measure longitude from a line running through Greenwich, England.

Manioc
A plant grown in the tropics, whose starchy roots are eaten as food.

Maroon
To leave someone behind on an island or coast during a sea voyage.

Mercury program
The first U.S. manned spaceflight program, which ran from 1959 to 1963.

Mid-Atlantic Ridge
An undersea mountain range that runs down the center of the Atlantic Ocean, from the Arctic to the Antarctic.

Ming
A Chinese dynasty, or family of rulers. The Ming dynasty ruled China from 1368 to 1644.

Mongols
A warlike people from Mongolia that conquered a huge empire in Asia in the 13th century.

Monsoon
A wind that changes direction in different seasons.

Mutiny
A rebellion against someone in authority, particularly by sailors against their captain.

NASA
The National Aeronautics and Space Administration, which was set up in 1958 by the U.S. government to run its space exploration program.

Naturalist
A scientist who studies animals and plants.

Natural selection
The means by which new living species are created, according to Charles Darwin's theory of evolution. Within a species, certain individuals are born with features that help them survive to have offspring. The features passed on are said to be "selected by nature." Small changes build up over time, and new species appear.

Navigation
The science of finding a way from one place to another.

Navigational instrument
A device, such as a magnetic compass or an astrolabe, used in navigation.

Northeast passage
A sea route from Europe over the top of Russia to the Pacific Ocean and Asia.

Northwest passage
A sea route from Europe over the top of North America to the Pacific Ocean and Asia.

Oceanography
The science of the oceans. This includes the study of marine life, currents, waves, weather, and the movements of Earth's crust.

Phoenicians
An ancient seafaring and trading people, whose homeland was on the coast of modern-day Lebanon.

Pilot
A skilled navigator.

Plateau
An area of high, flat land.

Poles
The points at the top and bottom of Earth, around which it revolves.

Prester John
A legendary Christian king thought to live somewhere in Africa or Asia during the Middle Ages. He was believed to be immensely rich and powerful.

Saga
A long story written for entertainment during the Middle Ages. Icelandic sagas are our main source of evidence of Viking exploration.

Sargasso Sea
A seaweed-covered area in the middle of the Atlantic Ocean.

Satellite
An artificial object orbiting Earth or another planetary body.

Scurvy
A disease caused by a lack of vitamin C, once common on long expeditions when fresh food ran out.

Seismic exploration
A method of exploring underground, using artificially created shock waves. Seismic exploration is used to search for gas and oil deposits.

Sherpas
The native people of the southern side of the Himalayan Mountains, in Nepal and India. Sherpas are excellent climbers and mountain guides.

Silk Road
A collection of trade routes from China to the Mediterranean. Many merchants traveled along it to buy silk from China.

Skraelings
The name given by Vikings to the Native Americans that they encountered. It is thought to come from their word *skra* (skin). Unlike the Vikings, who wore clothes of woven wool, Skraelings dressed in animal skins.

Snowmobile
A vehicle for traveling over snow and ice. It is propelled by tracks at the back and steered by skis at the front.

Sonar
The use of sound waves to locate objects by the echoes that they send back. Ships and submarines use sonar to detect underwater objects.

Space probe
An unmanned spacecraft sent into space to study other planets and moons.

Spices
The seeds, leaves, or bark of plants used to flavor food.

Sputnik
The name given to a series of robotic spacecraft, which were launched into orbit by the U.S.S.R. between 1957 and 1962. Sputnik 1 was the first satellite. Sputnik 2 carried a dog named Laika.

Strait
A narrow passage of water joining two large areas of water.

Terra Australis Incognita
The name given to a continent once wrongly believed to exist in the Southern Hemisphere. The name means "Unknown Southern land".

Thule
A northern land—probably Iceland or Norway—visited by the Ancient Greek explorer Pytheas.

U.S.S.R.
The Union of Soviet Socialist Republics (or Soviet Union) was a Eurasian state, dominated by Russia. It existed from 1922 until it fell apart in 1991.

Vikings
The seafaring people of Scandinavia, who lived between the 8th and 11th centuries.

Vostok program
A USSR space program that ran from 1961 and sent the first man and woman into space.

Wallace Line
A boundary dividing the animals and plants of East and West Malaya. It is named after the Victorian naturalist Alfred Russell Wallace.

White Nile
The White Nile is the longer of the two rivers that join together to form the Nile River.

I'm going to bone up on my definitions

I wouldn't fly over this part

Sonar yet so far

Arr, who be the captain of this ship?

I've clouded my view

INDEX

It's magical!

It's time to travel some more

Acknowledgments

Dorling Kindersley would like to thank Caitlin Doyle for proofreading, Jackie Brind for the index, Megan Lucas for editorial assistance, and Millie Popovic for design assistance.

Some Brainwaves were injured in the making of this book, but they have now fully recovered.